The **Earth** **Beneath** Our **Feet**

an earth science unit for high-ability learners in grades 3–4

The Earth Beneath Our Feet

Kimberley Thoresen
and Kimberley L. Chandler, Ph. D.

The College of William and Mary
School of Education
Center for Gifted Education
P.O. Box 8795
Williamsburg, VA 23187

Routledge
Taylor & Francis Group
NEW YORK AND LONDON

First published in 2014 by Prufrock Press Inc.

Published 2021 by Routledge
605 Third Avenue, New York, NY 10017
2 Park Square, Milton Park, Abingdon, Oxon OX14 4RN

Routledge is an imprint of the Taylor & Francis Group, an informa business

Production design by Raquel Trevino

ISBN 13: 978-1-0321-4151-0 (hbk)
ISBN 13: 978-1-6182-1045-6 (pbk)

DOI: 10.4324/9781003238775

Contents

Acknowledgements

Thanks to Pamela N. Harris and Lori Andersen, Ph.D.,
who acted as editorial assistants for this unit.

Part One: Unit Overview

DOI: 10.4324/9781003238775-1

Introduction to the Unit

The Earth Beneath Our Feet is a science unit designed to be used with high-ability third and fourth graders. Children are fascinated with soil. They enjoy digging in the ground and take pleasure in finding things like worms, insects, fossils, and rocks within the soil. This unit builds on the excitement that students have about investigating soil by engaging students in hands-on scientific investigations. Students in third and fourth grade begin to investigate and understand the major components of soil, its origin, and the important role it plays for humans. This unit works to expand on the content knowledge that students will develop by also including information about erosion and its impact on the land. Students participate in a variety of activities that expose them to the impact of natural and manmade processes on the weathering and erosion of rocks and soil. They also study the contemporary issue of fracking and why it is a controversial practice.

Curriculum Framework

The curriculum framework (see Table 1) is based on the Integrated Curriculum Model (ICM), which posits the relatively equal importance of teaching to high-level content, higher order processes and resultant products, and important concepts and issues. The model represents a research-based set of differentiated curricular and instructional approaches found appropriate for high-ability learners (VanTassel-Baska, 1986; VanTassel-Baska & Little, 2003). The framework serves several important functions:

1. The curriculum framework provides scaffolding for the central concept of change, the scientific research process, and the content of the units.
2. The curriculum framework also provides representative statements of advanced, complex, and sophisticated learner outcomes. It demonstrates how a single set of outcomes for all can be translated appropriately for high-ability learners yet can remain accessible to other learners.
3. The curriculum framework provides a way for readers to get a snapshot view of the key emphases of the curriculum in direct relation to each other. The model also provides a way to traverse the elements individually through the continuum of grade levels.
4. The curriculum framework provides information for students to be able to debate the potential advantages or disadvantages of the practice of hydraulic fracturing (fracking).

Standards Alignment

Each lesson was aligned to the appropriate Next Generation Science Standards (NGSS). Table 2 presents detailed information on the alignment between the NGSS and fundamental concepts within the unit lessons.

Macroconcept

The macroconcept for this unit is *change*. A concept paper on change is included in Appendix A. The second lesson in this unit introduces the concept of change. Students are asked to brainstorm examples of change, categorize their examples, identify "non-

DOI: 10.4324/9781003238775-2

Table 1

Curriculum Framework

Goal	**Student Outcomes** ***The student will be able to:***
1. Develop concepts related to understanding the world of science.	• Provide examples, illustrations, and salient features of important science and math concepts. • Categorize and/or classify various concepts. • Identify counterexamples of specific concepts. • Create definitions and generalizations about various concepts.
2. Develop an understanding of the macroconcept of change as it relates to science content goals.	• Understand that change is everywhere. • Demonstrate the impact of time on change. • Articulate the nature of natural versus manmade change. • Evaluate the nature of change (predictable or random) in selected phenomena.
3. Develop knowledge of selected content topics in Earth science.	• Understand how rocks are classified. • Understand the processes through which rocks can be changed from one type to another. • Describe and distinguish between weathering and erosion. • Articulate the factors that affect the formation of soil. • Articulate and describe the components of soil. • Name and describe the layers of soil. • Describe topsoil and articulate its importance. • Describe the negative and positive effects of erosion. • Describe why fracking is a controversial practice.
4. Develop interrelated science process skills.	• Make observations. • Ask questions. • Learn more. • Design and conduct an experiment. • Create meaning. • Tell others what was found.
5. Develop critical thinking skills.	• Describe problematic situations or issues. • Define relevant concepts. • Identify different points of view in situations or issues. • Describe evidence or data supporting a scientific question. • Draw conclusions based on data (making inferences). • Predict consequences.
6. Develop creative thinking skills.	• Develop fluency when naming objects and ideas. • Develop flexible thinking. • Elaborate on ideas presented in oral or written form. • Create products that replicate and extend conceptual understanding.
7. Develop curiosity and interest in the world of science.	• Express reactions about discrepant events. • Ask meaningful questions about science topics. • Articulate ideas of interest about science. • Demonstrate persistence in completing science tasks.

Table 2

Alignment to Next Generation Science Standards

Lesson	Next Generation Science Standards Met
Preteaching Lesson	N/A
Lesson 1: Preassessment	N/A
Lesson 2: What Is a Scientist?	N/A
Lesson 3: The Concept of Change	N/A
Lesson 4: Becoming a Geologist	N/A
Lesson 5: Rock Detectives	MS-ESS2-1: Develop a model to describe the cycling of Earth's materials and the flow of energy that drives this process.
Lesson 6: Changing Rocks	4-ESS2-1: Make observations and/or measurements to provide evidence of the effects of weathering or the rate of erosion by water, ice, wind, or vegetation.
Lesson 7: Soil Formation	4-ESS2-1: Make observations and/or measurements to provide evidence of the effects of weathering or the rate of erosion by water, ice, wind, or vegetation.
Lesson 8: Components of Soil	4-ESS2-1: Make observations and/or measurements to provide evidence of the effects of weathering or the rate of erosion by water, ice, wind, or vegetation.
Lesson 9: Soil Horizons	4-ESS2-1: Make observations and/or measurements to provide evidence of the effects of weathering or the rate of erosion by water, ice, wind, or vegetation.
Lesson 10: Plants and Soil	5-LS2-1: Develop a model to describe the movement of matter among plants, animals, decomposers, and the environment.
Lesson 11: Erosion	4-ESS2-1: Make observations and/or measurements to provide evidence of the effects of weathering or the rate of erosion by water, ice, wind, or vegetation.
Lesson 12: Erosion as Change	4-ESS2-1: Make observations and/or measurements to provide evidence of the effects of weathering or the rate of erosion by water, ice, wind, or vegetation.
Lesson 13: Erosion Prevention	5-ESS3-1: Obtain and combine information about ways individual communities use science ideas to protect the Earth's resources and environment.
Lesson 14: Contemporary Issue: Fracking	5-ESS3-1: Obtain and combine information about ways individual communities use science ideas to protect the Earth's resources and environment.
Lesson 15: Persuasive Writing	5-ESS3-1: Obtain and combine information about ways individual communities use science ideas to protect the Earth's resources and environment.
Lesson 16: Putting It All Together	N/A
Lesson 17: Postassessment	N/A

examples" of the concept, and make generalizations about the concept (Taba, 1962). The generalizations about change incorporated into this unit of study include:

- Change is everywhere.
- Change relates to time.
- Change can be natural or manmade.
- Change may be random or predictable.

The concept of change is integrated throughout the unit lessons and deepens students' understanding of natural resources and how resources may change. Students examine the relationship of important ideas and issues about natural resources through application of the concept generalizations. This higher level thinking enhances the students' ability to "think like a scientist." More information about concept development is provided in Appendix B: Teaching Models.

Before you begin, you may choose to use the preteaching lesson on safety in the science classroom, Science Safety (pp. 18–19), located prior to the preassessment lesson. Simulating the work of real scientists, students develop a systematic set of inquiry skills. As scientists, students must learn the basic safety precautions that are necessary while performing experiments of different natures. This optional lesson is designed to outline the importance of safety in the classroom. Science safety guidelines for teachers are also provided in this lesson.

Key Science Concepts

By the end of this unit, students will understand that:

1. Rocks are classified into three general categories based on the process by which they were formed: igneous, metamorphic, and sedimentary. Through processes such as weathering, erosion, sedimentation, heat, and pressure, rocks can be changed from one type to another.
2. Rocks are broken down by weathering, and the resulting particles are carried away by erosion.
3. The formation of soil is affected by multiple factors that include topography, climate, geology, time, and biological factors.
4. Rock, clay, silt, sand, and humus are components of soil. Different mixtures of these components create different kinds of soil. Clay, silt, and sand are all tiny bits of rock that are classified by particle size. Humus is decayed organic matter.
5. Soil has layers which include topsoil, subsoil, and bedrock. At any location, the characteristics of the soil depend on the type of bedrock present. Topsoil has the highest proportion of humus because the decaying plant matter lies directly on it.
6. Topsoil is needed to support plant life. Topsoil retains moisture, provides physical support for plant structure, and provides nutrients.
7. Erosion is the carrying away or movement of rock, soil, and sediments. Erosion is caused by agents of wind, water, ice, and gravity.
8. People can take steps to decrease the rate of erosion that occurs both naturally and due to human impact on the land. Erosion has negative and positive effects. For example, some of the most fertile soil in the world is in the Mississippi Delta and was created by deposition of eroded materials.
9. Fracking is the fracturing of rock by pressurized liquid. It allows liquids such as petroleum, groundwater, and gas to move into wells, but is controversial because of its potential impact on the environment.

Practice in using concept maps supports students' learning as they begin to build upon known concepts (Novak & Gowin, 1984). Students begin to add new concepts to their initial understandings of a topic and to make new connections between concepts. The use of concept maps within the lessons also helps teachers to recognize students' conceptual frameworks so that instruction can be adapted as necessary. More information on strategies for using concept mapping, as well as a list of concept mapping practice activities, is provided in Appendix B. This unit also contains a science concept map (see Figure 1) that displays the essential understandings and the connections students should be able to make as a result of their experiences within the unit. This overview

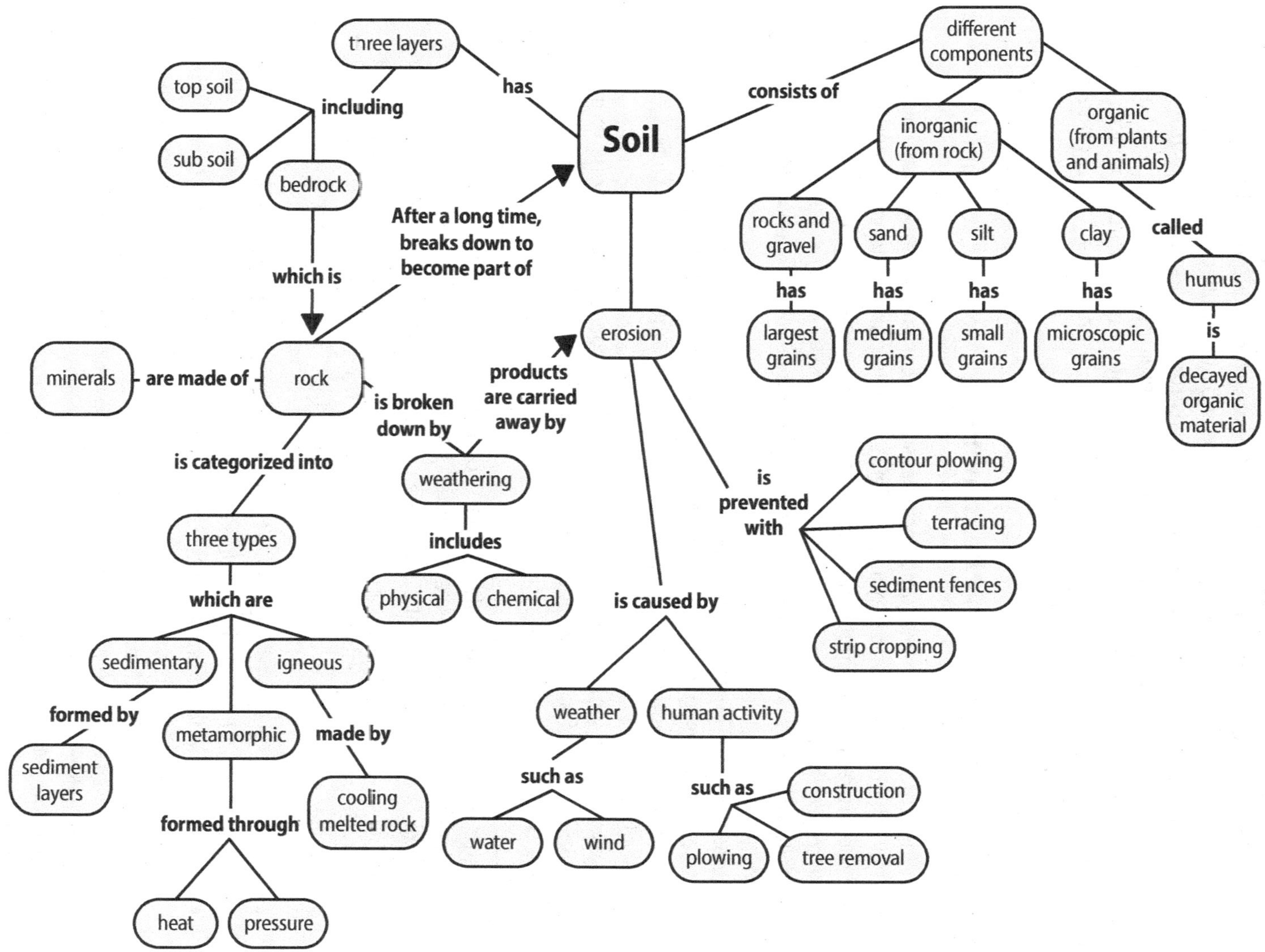

Figure 1. Soil concept map.

may be useful as a classroom poster that teachers and students can refer to throughout the unit.

In addition to the concept map, teachers also will notice references to a "word wall" in the unit. The word wall is suggested for use in the classroom while teaching the unit. On this wall, teachers will post or write words (and their definitions) that go along with the lessons. Use the definitions listed in the Unit Glossary for the word wall; you also can use additional vocabulary from the lessons that may be unfamiliar to the students on the word wall. At the end of the unit, teachers are instructed to assign words from the word wall to student groups for an activity that involves students creating word demonstrations. Teachers can assess students' understanding of each word or concept by the quality of understanding demonstrated in students' presentations. A list of materials needed for the unit is provided in Appendix C.

Scientific Investigation and Reasoning

The Wheel of Scientific Investigation and Reasoning contains the specific processes involved in scientific inquiry that guide students' thinking and actions. To read more about these processes and suggestions for implementing the wheel in this unit's lessons, see Appendix B.

The following lessons utilize the components Wheel of Scientific Investigation and Reasoning:

- Lessons 6, 10, 11, and 13, which help students explore the six components of scientific investigation including: Make Observations, Ask Questions, Learn More, Design and Conduct Experiments, Create Meaning, and Tell Others What Was Found.
- Lessons 5–14, which provide opportunities for students to apply one or more components of scientific investigation and culminate with an in-depth scientific investigation.

Students use the wheel to analyze aspects of an investigation or to plan an investigation. Scientific investigation concepts within the lessons include:

- *Make Observations*: Scientists use their senses as well as instruments to note details, identify similarities and differences, and record changes in phenomena.
- *Ask Questions*: Scientists use information from their observations about familiar objects or events to develop important questions that spark further investigation.
- *Learn More*: Scientists carefully review what is known about a topic and determine what additional information must be sought.
- *Design and Conduct Experiments*: Scientists design an experiment, which is a fair test of a hypothesis or prediction and is intended to answer a question for a scientific investigation.
- *Create Meaning*: Scientists carefully gather and record data from an experiment, then analyze the data.
- *Tell Others What Was Found*: Scientists communicate findings from an experiment, including a clear description of the question, the hypothesis or prediction, the experiment that was conducted, the data that were collected and how they were analyzed, and the conclusions and inferences that were made from the experiment.

Assessment

The unit includes performance-based assessments for students to complete at the beginning (preassessment) and end (postassessment) of the unit. There are three pre- and postassessments, which assess conceptual understanding, science content knowledge, and application of the scientific investigation process. The preassessment provides baseline data that teachers can use to adjust instructional plans for individual students or groups of students. Preteaching activities accompany selected preassessments.

The postassessment is administered at the completion of the unit and provides valuable information about students' mastery of the targeted objectives and the Next Generation Science Standards. A rubric is used to score each pre- and postassessment. The pre- and postassessments and dimensions of learning scored for each task include:

- *A macroconcept template, which requires students to draw or write about the macroconcept.* Conceptual understanding is scored on the pre- and postassessments based on the number of appropriate examples of the macroconcept, the elements of the macroconcept, types of the macroconcept listed, and generalizations about the macroconcept.
- *Concept maps, which assess students' content knowledge.* Students are given a prompt for creating a concept map about the unit topic. Understanding of key science concepts is scored on the pre- and postassessments based on the number of appropriate hierarchical levels, propositions, and examples listed.
- *An experimental design template, which requires students to plan an experiment with a given scientific research question.* Students are asked to design an experiment to investigate a question. Students are scored on the pre- and postassessments on their ability to write a prediction or hypothesis, list materials needed for the experiment, list the steps of the experiment in order, and develop a plan to organize data for collection and interpretation.

Teachers also should note that assessment "Look Fors" are designated in the first section of each lesson plan. The "Look Fors" provide a means for teachers to assess student learning in each lesson. The "Look Fors" are linked to the macroconcept generalizations, key science concepts, and scientific processes identified in each lesson. Teachers can develop checklists for the "Look Fors" or may make informal observations, for example.

Teacher's Guide to Content

This unit teaches students about rocks, weathering and erosion, soil, and how erosion can be prevented. Weathering and erosion work together to break down rock and create soil, but these categories of processes have distinct differences. Weathering occurs through two processes that often work together to decompose rocks that are called mechanical and chemical weathering. There is no movement of the rock material during these processes. Weathering occurs on or near the surface of the rock. First, chemical weathering occurs when a chemical change occurs in some of the minerals within the rock. For example, rocks such as limestone will react chemically with carbonic acid (naturally present in rain) to form calcium bicarbonate. Second, mechanical weathering occurs when rocks are physically broken into pieces without any chemical change of the minerals within the rock. One example of mechanical weathering is repeated thawing and freezing. For example, when the weather is warm, water seeps into the cracks in rocks. When the temperature gets cold enough, the water turns to ice. Water expands the cracks in the rock as it freezes, eventually breaking the rock. An important aspect of weathering is that the rock pieces do not move.

In contrast, erosion occurs when a flowing agent, such as air, water, or ice, carries particles. An example of erosion is the action of wind. When wind blows, it can blow sand, soil, and rocks against larger rocks, wearing the surface of the larger rock away like sandpaper. It is important to remember that if a particle is loosened but stays put, it is called weathering. When the particle starts moving, it is called erosion.

Soil is much more than bits of rock. Soil composition is characteristic of a geographic region because broken-down native bedrock becomes a part of the soil. Fertile soil also contains organic matter. The top layer on the ground consists of leaves that have fallen from trees, or other dead plant or animal material that has decayed on the ground. These components eventually form humus, a black, sticky, nutrient-rich material found beneath the top layer. The uppermost layer of soil is called topsoil, and is generally dark and crumbly. The topsoil is the most fertile layer of the soil because it contains the most humus. It can range in depth from a few centimeters to a meter. Below the topsoil is a lighter brown layer of subsoil. Subsoil contains less water and humus to offer plants. Underneath the subsoil is partially broken-down rock. The rock fragments are from the more solid layer of parent rock below.

Erosion removes topsoil and has negative impacts on farming. The rate of soil erosion depends on multiple factors including climate, geological factors, and biological factors. Erosion can be prevented by a variety of methods, such as strip cropping, contour plowing, terracing, no-till methods, and replanting forests. Erosion prevention is an important topic because the loss of topsoil affects the ability to grow crops. However, erosion can have positive effects, such as the creation of fertile regions like the Mississippi Delta.

Fracking is the fracturing of rock by pressurized liquid. It allows liquids such as petroleum, groundwater, and gas to move into wells, but is controversial because of its potential impact on the environment.

DOI: 10.4324/9781003238775-3

Unit Glossary

Bedrock: unbroken solid rock, overlaid in most places by soil or rock fragments.

Clay: a mineral particle of any composition that has a grain size smaller than 1/256 mm. Clay is plastic or slippery when wet and can be rolled into a long, snake-shaped strand.

Contour plowing: plowing the land perpendicular to rather than parallel to slopes and hills. When this is done, the soil follows the contours of the land.

Erosion: the process by which the surface of the Earth is worn away and moved by the action of water, glaciers, wind, waves, etc.

Fracking: the fracturing of rock by pressurized liquid.

Geologist: a person who studies the science that deals with the dynamics and physical history of the Earth, the rocks of which it is composed, and the physical, chemical, and biological changes that the Earth has undergone or is undergoing.

Gravel: a mineral particle of any composition that has a grain size larger than 2 mm.

Horizon: a layer of soil that differs in color and texture from the layers above or below it.

Humus: the dark portion of soil that consists of organic materials that are well enough decayed that the original source material cannot be identified.

Igneous Rock: rock formed by the crystallization of magma or lava.

Loam: a rich soil containing a relatively equal mixture of sand and silt and a somewhat smaller proportion of clay.

Metamorphic rock: rock that was once one form of rock but has changed to another under the influence of heat, pressure, or some other agent without passing through a liquid phase.

Mineral: solid, natural, and inorganic material, usually having a definite chemical composition and a characteristic atomic structure.

Natural resource: naturally occurring material that can be used by living organisms to meet a specific need.

Rock: solid matter made of minerals.

Sand: a mineral particle of any composition that has a grain size smaller than 2 mm but larger than 1/16 mm. Sand feels gritty; it holds together when wet but crumbles easily.

Sedimentary rock: rock formed from the accumulation of sediment. Sediment particles include clay, silt, sand, and gravel.

Silt: a mineral particle of any composition that has a grain size larger than 1/256 mm but smaller than 1/16 mm. Silt feels smooth and silky between the fingers; it holds together when wet and does not crumble easily; it cannot be rolled into a long, snake-shaped strand.

Soil: the loose material in which plants can grow in the upper layer of the Earth. It is a mixture of rock, sand, clay, silt, and humus.

Strip cropping: planting strips of thick grass or clover between strips of crops.

Subsoil: the layer under the topsoil.

Tilling: preparing land for crops by plowing and harrowing; cultivating.

DOI: 10.4324/9781003238775-4

Topsoil: the top layer of soil that is made up of the smallest pieces of rock. It has the most humus and is the most fertile layer of soil.

Weathering: the chemical or physical process by which rocks are broken down into smaller pieces at the Earth's surface.

Teaching Resources

Annenberg Learning. (2011). *Earth and space science session 1: Earth's solid membrane: Soil.* Retrieved from http://www.learner.org/courses/essential/earthspace/session 1/index.html#

Bosak, S. V. (2000). *Science is . . .* (2nd ed.). Toronto, Ontario: Scholastic Canada Ltd.

Daniel, L. H., Hackett, J., Moyer, R. H., Baptiste, H. P., Stryker, P., & Vasquez, J. (2002). *Science teacher's edition: Earth science unit c.* New York, NY: Macmillan/McGraw-Hill.

Estigarribia, D. (2005). *Learning about rocks, weathering, and erosion with graphic organizers.* New York, NY: PowerKids Press.

Jones, R. M., McLeod, J. C., Krockover, G. H., Frank, M. J., Lang, M. P., Valenta, C. J., & Van Deman, B. A. (2002). *Science teacher's edition: Earth science unit c.* Orlando, FL: Harcourt.

Kardos, T. (1997). *75 easy Earth science demonstrations.* Portland, ME: J. Weston Walch.

Lehn, B. (1998). *What is a scientist?* Brookfield, CN: The Millbrook Press.

Parrella, D. (1995). *Project seasons.* Shelburne, VT: Shelburne Farms.

Strahler, A., & Strahler, A. (2005). *Physical geography: Science and systems of the human environment* (3rd ed.). Hoboken, NJ: John Wiley & Sons.

Sunal, D. W., & Sunal, C. S. (2003). *Science in the elementary and middle school.* Upper Saddle River, NJ: Pearson Education.

Tolman, M. N. (1995). *Hands-on Earth science activities for grades K–8.* West Nyack, NY: Parker.

Student Resources

Bailey, J. (2006). *Cracking up: A story about erosion.* Minneapolis, MN: Picture Window Books.

Bail, R. (2000). *A handful of dirt.* New York, NY: Walker Books.

Ditchfield, C. (2003). *Soil.* Chicago, IL: Children's Press.

Fuller, S. (2003). *Rocks and minerals.* New York, NY: DK Publishing.

Gurnery, B. (2005). *Sand and soil: Earth's building blocks.* New York, NY: Crabtree.

Harman, R. (2005). *Rock cycles.* Chicago, IL: Heinemann Library.

Hiscock, B. (1988). *The big rock.* New York, NY: Aladdin Paperbacks.

Kellert, S. (Ed.). (1997). *Macmillan encyclopedia of the environment.* New York, NY: Macmillan.

Kittinger, J. S. (1998). *A look at rocks: From coal to kimberlite.* New York, NY: Scholastic.

Markle, S. (1991). *Earth alive!* New York, NY: Lothrop, Lee, & Shepard.

Moriss, N. (1998). *Rocks and minerals.* New York, NY: Crabtree.

Pellant, C. (2002). *Smithsonian handbooks: Rocks and minerals.* New York, NY: DK Publishing.

Peters, L. (1998). *The sun, the wind, and the rain.* New York, NY: Henry Holt.

Silverstein, A., & Silverstein, V. (2000). *Life in a bucket of soil.* New York, NY: Dover.

Tomeneck, S. (2002). *Dirt: Jump into science.* Washington, DC: National Geographic Children's Books.

DOI: 10.4324/9781003238775-5

Useful Websites

Dictionary.com. (2014). Retrieved from http://dictionary.reference.com

Discovery Education's United Streaming. (2014). Retrieved from http://www.unitedstreaming.com

Full Option Science System. (2014). *Rock database*. Retrieved from http://archive.fossweb.com/modules3-6/EarthMaterials/activities/rockdatabase/index.html

Geography4Kids.com. (2013). *Covering the lithosphere*. Retrieved from http://www.geography4kids.com/files/land_soil.html

Geography4Kids.com. (2013). *Makin' the soil*. Retrieved from http://www.geography4kids.com/files/land_soil2.html

Geography4Kids.com. (2013). *Rocks and minerals*. Retrieved from http://www.geography4kids.com/files/earth_rocktypes.html

Gliffy. (2013). *Diagrams made* easy. Retrieved from http://www.gliffy.com

Google Earth. (2013). Retrieved from http://earth.google.com

NASA. (2014). *Soil science education*. Retrieved from http://soils.gsfc.nasa.gov

National Resources Conservation Service. (2014). Retrieved from http://www.nrcs.usda.gov/wps/portal/nrcs/site/national/home/

Ohio State University. (2008). *Beyond penguins and polar bears*. Retrieved from http://beyondpenguins.ehe.osu.edu/issue/earths-changing-surface/the-forces-that-change-the-face-of-earth

Smithsonian Institution. (2014). *Dig it! The secrets of soil*. Retrieved from http://forces.si.edu/soils/

Smithsonian Institution. (2014). *The dynamic Earth*. Retrieved from http://www.mnh.si.edu/earth

United States Department of Agriculture. (2010). *From the surface down*. Retrieved from ftp://ftp-fc.sc.egov.usda.gov/NSSC/Educational_Resources/surdown.pdf

Part Two: Lesson Plans

DOI: 10.4324/9781003238775-6

Overview of Lessons

An overview of the lessons is provided in Table 3. The overview shows the primary emphasis of each lesson in the unit according to the macroconcept, key science concepts, or the scientific investigation process. Lessons may also have a secondary emphasis, which is listed in the planning section of each lesson.

Lesson Plan Blueprint

In planning to incorporate these lessons in your classroom, you might find the blueprint included in Table 4 helpful. This table breaks down each lesson, detailing the instructional purpose, essential science understandings, scientific investigation skills and processes, generalizations about the overarching concept of change, and the basic concepts emphasized in the unit.

Table 3

Overview of Lessons

Concept of Change	Scientific Process	Key Science Concepts
Lesson 1: Preassessment		
	Lesson 2: What Is a Scientist?	
Lesson 3: The Concept of Change		
	Lesson 4: Becoming a Geologist	
	Lesson 5: Rock Detectives	
	Lesson 6: Changing Rocks	
	Lesson 7: Soil Formation	
	Lesson 8: Components of Soil	
		Lesson 9: Soil Horizons
	Lesson 10: Plants and Soil	
	Lesson 11: Erosion	
Lesson 12: Erosion as Change		
		Lesson 13: Erosion Prevention
		Lesson 14: Contemporary Issue: Fracking
Lesson 15: Persuasive Writing		
Lesson 16: Putting It All Together		
Lesson 17: Postassessment		

 DOI: 10.4324/9781003238775-7

Table 4

Lesson Plan Blueprint

Lesson #	Title	Instructional Purpose	Essential Science Understandings	Key Science Concepts	Change Generalizations
1	Preassessment	• To determine students' prior knowledge of unit content. • To assess student knowledge of the scientific process. • To assess student understanding of the concept of change.			
2	What Is a Scientist?	• To learn the characteristics of scientists and the investigation skills that scientists use.		• Make observations. • Ask questions. • Learn more. • Design and conduct experiments. • Create meaning. • Tell others what was found.	
3	The Concept of Change	• To understand the concept of change and develop generalizations about the concept of change.	• Scientists detect change with their senses.	• Make observations.	• Change is everywhere. • Change is related to time. • Change can be natural or manmade. • Change can be random or predictable.
4	Becoming a Geologist	• To explore the characteristics of a particular type of scientist: a geologist. • To define geology.	• The Earth's surface changes continuously over time. • Geologists study changes in the Earth.	• Make observations. • Ask questions. • Learn more. • Design and conduct experiments. • Create meaning from the experiment. • Tell others what was found.	• Geologists study manmade and natural changes in the Earth that occur over time. • Some of these changes are random and some are predictable. • Changes occur everywhere on the surface of the Earth.
5	Rock Detectives	• To apply the steps of the Wheel of Scientific Investigation and Reasoning.	• There are three types of rock. • Rocks are made up of minerals. • Rocks change due to various processes.	• Make observations. • Ask questions. • Learn more.	• The processes by which rocks are formed are natural changes that occur over time.

Table 4, *continued*

Lesson #	Title	Instructional Purpose	Essential Science Understandings	Key Science Concepts	Change Generalizations
6	Changing Rocks	• To engage students in scientific investigations. • To conduct experiments to explore weathering and erosion.	• Weathering refers to the mechanical and chemical processes that decompose rock, while erosion is the process by which those rock particles are carried away by wind or water. • One component of soil is small pieces of rock.	• Make observations. • Ask questions. • Learn more. • Create meaning. • Tell others what was found.	• Weathering and erosion are examples of natural changes. • Weathering and erosion take time to occur.
7	Soil Formation	• To engage students in the research processes by gathering information about soil from a variety of sources.	• The formation of soil is affected by multiple factors. • One component of soil is small pieces of rock. • It takes thousands of years for rocks to break down into soil.	• Ask questions. • Learn more. • Tell others what was found.	• The process of weathering takes a long time.
8	Components of Soil	• To investigate characteristics of different soils. • To identify soil layers (horizons).	• Soil provides support and nutrients for plants. • Rock, clay, silt, sand, and humus are the five components of soil. Rock, clay, silt, and sand come from the weathering of bedrock. Humus comes from the decay of organic material. • Different mixtures of the five components result in different kinds of soil that are characteristic to a location.	• Make observations. • Ask questions. • Learn more.	• All of the inorganic components of soil are the results of a process of change called weathering. The organic component of soil comes from a process of change called decomposition. These processes occur over time.
9	Soil Horizons	• To identify soil layers (horizons).	• There are three layers of soil, or soil horizons: topsoil, subsoil, and bedrock. • Bedrock is turned into rocks, gravel, sand, silt, and clay through weathering.	• Make observations. • Ask questions. • Learn more.	• Soil horizons are evidence of changes occurring within the Earth.
10	Plants and Soil	• To investigate different types of soil and evaluate the effectiveness of each type for supporting plant life.	• Soil provides support and nutrients for plants. • The composition of the soil affects how well it supports plant life.	• Make observations. • Ask questions. • Learn more. • Design and conduct experiments. • Create meaning. • Tell others what was found.	• Changes to the composition of the soil affect how well plant life is supported.
11	Erosion	• To investigate soil erosion, the negative effects of erosion, and ways to prevent erosion.	• Over time, rocks break down and become part of the soil. • Topsoil is formed over a long period of time from the weathering of bedrock and subsoil. • Erosion is when rock, soil, and sediment are carried away. Erosion is caused by wind, water, ice, and gravity.	• Make observations. • Ask questions. • Learn more. • Design and conduct experiments. • Create meaning. • Tell others what was found.	• Erosion is an example of natural change that can be sped up or slowed down by things that people do.

Table 4, *continued*

Lesson #	Title	Instructional Purpose	Essential Science Understandings	Key Science Concepts	Change Generalizations
12	Erosion as Change	• To understand the application of change generalizations to erosion.	• Erosion can be natural or caused by man. • Erosion is related to the four change generalizations. • Erosion has positive and negative results. • Erosion can be fast or slow. The rate of erosion is affected by the topography.		• Erosion is an example of change that has positive and negative effects and can happen slowly or quickly. • The rate of erosion is affected by manmade and natural factors.
13	Erosion Prevention	• To develop students' abilities to research a specific problem.	• The rate of erosion depends on multiple factors, including climate, geological factors, and biological factors. • People can take steps to decrease the rate of erosion that occurs naturally and that is caused by human impacts on the land.	• Make observations. • Ask questions. • Learn more. • Design and conduct an experiment. • Tell others what was found.	• The rate of erosion can be slowed through various means.
14	Contemporary Issue: Fracking	• To determine the potential advantages and disadvantages of hydraulic fracturing (fracking). • To analyze and evaluate the evidence related to fracking.	• Hydraulic fracturing, or "fracking," is a process by which natural gas and oil are extracted from bedrock by opening and widening fractures below the Earth's surface and injecting a mixture of water, chemicals, and silica sand at high pressure into drilled wells in the Earth (United States Environmental Protection Agency, 2013). • Recent modern drilling techniques have made fracking an economical method to harvest natural gas and oil. There are many concerns about the environmental and health risks of fracking.	• Make observations. • Ask questions.	• Change can be natural or manmade.
15	Persuasive Writing	• To guide students in developing persuasive arguments about erosion.	• Some erosion is preventable. • There are many prevention methods that can be used to combat erosion, including strip cropping, contour plowing, terracing, no-till methods, and replanting forests.	• Create meaning. • Tell others.	• Controlling changes to the soil by erosion is important to the farming industry.
16	Putting It All Together	• To review the interrelationships between the concept of change, the scientific process, and unit science content.			
17	Postassessment	• To assess student knowledge of unit content, the scientific process, and the concept of change.			

Preteaching Lesson: Science Safety

Note: Please read the Science Safety Guidelines (Handout 0A, p. 20) prior to teaching this lesson.

Planning the Lesson

Instructional Purpose

- To instill in students the importance of safety in the classroom.
- To outline science safety rules to be implemented throughout the unit.

Instructional Time

- 45 minutes

Materials/Resources/Equipment

- Sample materials:
    - Soil
    - Plastic bag of nonhazardous powdery substance (e.g., sugar)
    - Closed jar of nonhazardous liquid (e.g., water)

- Plastic disposable gloves
- Safety goggles
- Chart paper
- Markers
- Copies of Handout 0A (Science Safety Guidelines)
- Poster of Handout 0B (Science Safety Rules)

Implementing the Lesson

1. Display sample materials on a long table in front of students and distribute copies of Handout 0A (Science Safety Guidelines). Inform students that they soon will begin a science unit in which they will observe and study many different kinds of materials, such as these. Explain that it is important for students to practice safety during the investigations. Relate the necessity of science safety rules to those of the classroom and physical education.
2. Display and define each item. Tell students that as a class, they will create a list of rules they should follow when handling these materials. Have students think of how they can keep their bodies safe. Record these examples on chart paper.
3. Next, unveil the Handout 0B (Science Safety Rules) on chart paper. Have students compare the two lists. How do students' examples relate to these rules? If necessary, add additional rules to the list.
4. Explain why some materials (e.g., knives) or elements (e.g., fire) are never appropriate for children to handle in school. Briefly discuss the potential hazards associated with these.
5. Finally, conduct a brief demonstration to illustrate how to practice safety guidelines. Take the plastic bag containing a nonhazardous powdery substance and the jar of nonhazardous liquid. Explain that you are going to investigate how

DOI: 10.4324/9781003238775-8

the two materials interact. Ask students how you can be safe while doing this investigation. Reinforce that substances can be harmful to the eyes or skin and that they should **never** be ingested. Explain that the same is true of soil, which can be toxic to humans. Emphasize that students should follow similar guidelines when studying soil.

6. Following students' examples of safety measures, demonstrate how to use safety goggles to protect the eyes, plastic gloves to protect the hands, and other relevant protective measures, such as pulling long hair back and wearing appropriate clothing. Conduct the demonstration by carefully pouring the powdery substance into the jar of liquid. Emphasize that you should never touch your face or mouth (and especially should not eat or drink) during science experiments.
7. Tell students that materials will be disposed of properly by the teacher after the investigation is completed. Students should not touch any potentially harmful substances.
8. Demonstrate the final rule, "Wash your hands," by properly removing the gloves (without the outside of the gloves ever touching the body) and the goggles. If there is a sink in the classroom, demonstrate how to properly wash one's hands. If no sink is present, inform students that after each investigation the class will go to the bathroom to wash their hands.
9. Conclude the lesson by emphasizing that science investigations are interesting and fun, but they also can be dangerous if not conducted properly. By following the Science Safety Rules, the class will enjoy the benefits of learning about science.

Name:____ Date: ____________________

Handout 0A
Science Safety Guidelines

1. Know and follow your school's policies and procedures regarding classroom safety.
2. Always provide direct adult supervision when students are engaging in scientific experimentation.
3. Ensure that all materials and equipment are safe for handling by primary students.
4. Exert extra caution when materials have the potential for harm when used improperly.
5. Use protective gear for eyes, skin, and breathing when conducting experiments, and require students to do the same.
6. Always conduct an experiment by yourself before completing it with the students.
7. Store materials for experiments out of the reach of students.
8. Never allow students to eat or drink during science experiments.
9. Follow general safety rules for sharp objects, heated items, breakables, or spilled liquids.
10. Teach students that it is unsafe to touch their face, mouth, eyes, or other body parts when they are working with plants, animals, microorganisms, or chemicals. Wash hands prior to touching anything. Caution students about putting anything in their mouth or breathing in the smell of substances.
11. Be aware of students' allergies to plants (including plant pollen), animals, foods, chemicals, or other substances to be used in the science classroom. Take all precautions necessary. Common food allergens include peanuts, tree nuts (cashews, almonds, walnuts, hazelnuts, macadamia nuts, pecans, pistachios, and pine nuts), shellfish, fish, milk, eggs, wheat, and soy.
12. Use caution with plants. Never allow students to pick or handle any unknown plants, leaves, flowers, seeds, or berries. Use gloves to touch unknown plants. Many common house, garden, and wooded area plants are toxic.
13. Avoid glass jars and containers. Use plastic, paper, or cloth containers.
14. Thermometers should be filled with alcohol, not mercury.
15. Clearly label any chemicals used and dispose of them properly.
16. Teach students safety rules for science (see Handout 0B), including:
    a. Always do scientific experiments with an adult present.
    b. Never mix things together (liquids, powders) without adult approval.
    c. Use your senses carefully. Protect your eyes, ears, nose, mouth, and skin.
    d. Wash your hands after using materials for an experiment.

Name:____________________________ Date: ________________

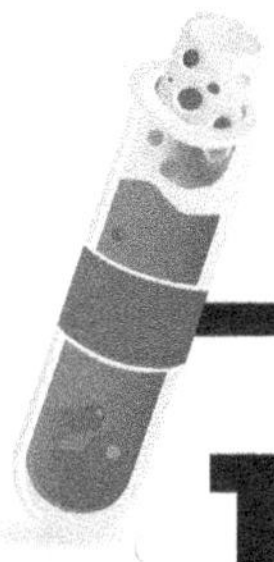

Handout 0B
Science Safety Rules

1 **Always** do scientific experiments with an adult present.

2 **Never** mix things together (liquids, powders) without adult approval.

3 **Use** your senses carefully. Protect your eyes, ears, nose, mouth, and skin.

4 **Wash your hands** after using materials for an experiment.

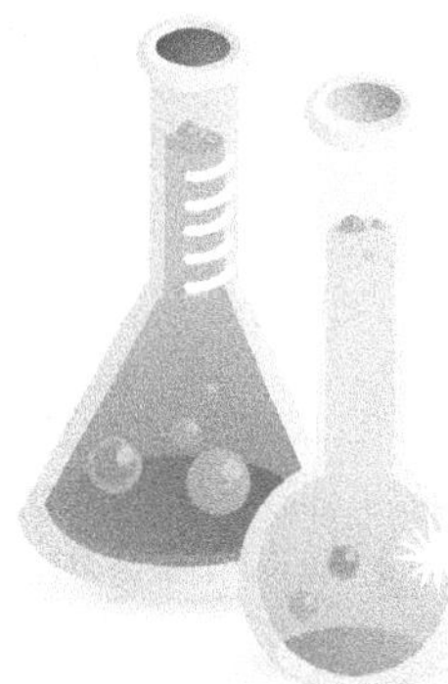

Lesson 1: Preassessment

Planning the Lesson

Instructional Purpose

- To determine prior knowledge of unit content.
- To build understanding of the unit macroconcept, science content, and science processes.

Instructional Time

- Macroconcept assessment: 20 minutes
- Key science concepts assessment: 30 minutes, including preteaching activity
- Scientific process assessment: 20 minutes

Materials/Resources/Equipment

- Copies of preassessments for the unit for each student: Handout 1A (Preassessment for Change Concept), Handout 1B (Concept Map: Soil), and Handout 1C (Preassessment for Scientific Process)
- Preteaching for Key Science Concepts Preassessment (p. 27) instructions for your use
- Rubrics 1–3 (Scoring Rubric for Change Concept, Scoring Rubric for Key Science Concepts, Scoring Rubric for Scientific Process) for your use
- Copy of Sample Concept Map (p. 31) for your use
- Pencils
- Large chart paper
- Drawing paper for each student
- Student logs (e.g., spiral or composition notebooks)

Implementing the Lesson

1. Explain to the students that they are beginning a new unit of study about the Earth beneath their feet. They will be completing three preassessments (Handouts 1A, 1B, and 1C) to determine what they already know about rocks, soil, change, and how to conduct experiments. Be sure the students know that you do not expect them to know all the answers for the preassessments. Tell the students that you will use the information from the preassessments to guide the planning of the unit lessons, and that they will know all of the answers by the end of the unit.
2. Collect the preassessments. Debrief with students to begin building their understanding of the unit concept, process, and content. Ask the students what was easy or difficult about the assessments. Briefly review each assessment and discuss some of the responses in general. Assure students that the unit will allow them to develop the knowledge and skills to do well on the assessment material.
3. Give each student a student log (e.g., a simple spiral or composition notebook). The logs will be used to keep records of all of their activities in this unit. Students will glue handouts into the log, respond to questions in the log, and keep notes from their experiments and research. Explain that scientists keep a log of their investigations and that they should date each entry that is put in the log. Have

DOI: 10.4324/9781003238775-9

students put the date on the first page and respond to the following statements related to the unit:

- I want to learn about . . .
- It is important to understand how nature and humans change things in the environment because . . .

4. Score the preassessments using the provided rubrics. Review the results of the preassessments to determine students' level of readiness for unit lessons and to guide grouping decisions.

Concluding and Ending the Lesson

What to Do at Home

- Have students think of a list of things scientists might study about rocks and soil. Have them generate questions that could be asked in the study and write the questions in their logs.

Name:________________________________ Date: ______________

Handout 1A
Preassessment for Change Concept

1. Give as many examples of things that change as you can (up to 10).

______________________	______________________
______________________	______________________
______________________	______________________
______________________	______________________
______________________	______________________

2. Draw one example of something that changes, showing before and after the change. Provide as many details as you can.

Before	**After**

3. Identify five ways that a tree could change or be changed.

____

____

____

____

____

4. What are three things you can say about *all* change?

All change ____________________________________

____

All change ____________________________________

____

All change ____________________________________

____

Name:______________________________ Date: ______________

Rubric 1
Scoring Rubric for Change Concept

Directions for Use: Score students on their completed preassessments.

		5	4	3	2	1	0
1	**Examples of the Concept**	At least 9–10 appropriate examples are given.	At least 7–8 appropriate examples are given.	At least 5–6 appropriate examples are given.	At least 3 appropriate examples are given.	At least 1–2 appropriate examples are given.	No examples are given.
2	**Drawing of Before-After**	The drawing contains five changed elements depicting a before-after situation.	The drawing contains four changed elements depicting a before-after situation.	The drawing contains three changed elements that depict a before-after situation.	The drawing contains two elements and does not clearly indicate a change relationship.	The drawing contains only one picture element or does not show a before-after relationship.	The drawing contains no elements.
3	**Types of Change**	Five different types of changes are identified.	Four different types of changes are identified.	Three different types of changes are identified.	Two different types of changes are identified.	One different type of change is identified.	No type of change is identified.
4	**Generalizations**	Reflects three appropriate generalizations about change.	Reflects three somewhat appropriate generalizations about change.	Reflects two appropriate generalizations about change.	Reflects one appropriate generalization about change.	Reflects only a statement about change.	No statements or generalizations about change are provided.

Total points possible: 20

Preteaching for Key Science Concepts Preassessment

Directions for the Teacher: Say the following bolded directions to students. Directions for you are not bolded.

Sometimes we know a lot about something even before our teachers teach it in school. Sometimes we don't know very much at all, but we like to learn new things.

For example, what would you think about if someone asked you to tell all you know about how *farms* work? What are some of the words you would use?

(List these on a chart.)

What are some of the things that happen on a farm?

(List these on a chart.)

I am going to show you a way I might tell all I know about how farms work.

(Begin a concept map on a large sheet of paper, using pictures and words, making simple links, and emphasizing these links.)

Make your own concept maps on your drawing paper. This practice activity can be done with a partner.

(Share some of the resulting concept maps, encouraging students to articulate their links.)

Preassessment for Key Science Concepts

Directions to the Teacher: Read the following paragraph to the students.

> Today I would like you to think about all of the things you know about soil. Think about the words you would use and the pictures you could draw to make a concept map. Think about the connections you can make. On your concept map paper, draw in pictures and words all that you know about soil. You will be drawing a concept map, just like the ones you did when we discussed the farm. Today's question is: "Tell me everything you know about soil."

Name:______________________________ Date: ______________

Handout 1B
Blank Concept Map

Name:______________________________ Date: ________________

Rubric 2
Scoring Rubric for Key Science Concepts

Directions for Use: Score students on their completed maps.

	5	4	3	2	1	0
Hierarchical Level Each subordinate concept is more specific and less general than the concept drawn above it. Count the number of levels included in the total map.	Five or more levels are identified.	Four levels are identified.	Three levels are identified.	Two levels are identified.	One level is identified.	No hierarchical levels are identified.
Propositions The linking of two concepts indicating a clear relationship is given. Count the total number of propositions identified on the total map.	Twelve or more propositions are provided.	Ten to 12 propositions are provided.	Seven to nine propositions are provided.	Four to six propositions are provided.	One to three propositions are provided.	No propositions are provided.
Examples A valid example of a concept is provided. Count the total number of examples.	Twelve or more examples are provided.	Ten to 12 examples are provided.	Seven to nine examples are provided.	Four to six examples are provided.	One to three examples are provided.	No examples are provided.

Total points possible: 15

Sample Concept Map

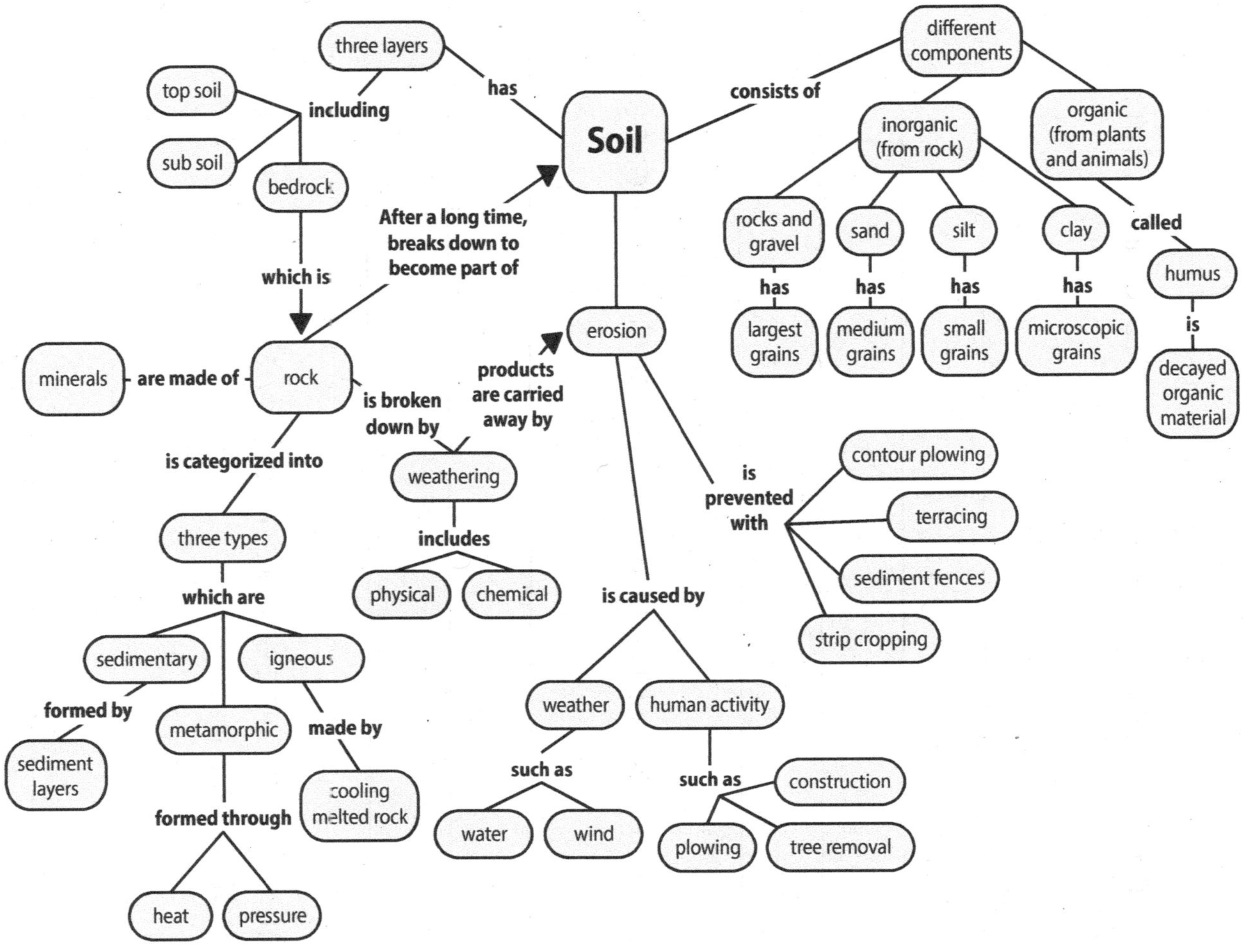

Name:____ Date: ____________________

Handout 1C
Preassessment for Scientific Process

Directions: How would you study the question: Are plants attracted to the sun? Describe an experiment to test this question that includes the following:

1. Prediction regarding the question (Are plants attracted to the sun?):

   I predict that ____

   ____

   ____

   ____

2. What materials will be needed to conduct the experiment?

   ____________________ ____________________

   ____________________ ____________________

   ____________________ ____________________

3. What steps must be taken to conduct the experiment and *in what order*?

   a. ____

   b. ____

   c. ____

   d. ____

   e. ____

4. What data do you want to collect and how should they be recorded?

What will I collect?	How will I record the data?

5. How do the data help me decide if my prediction is correct? Explain.

____

____

____

____

Name:______________________________ Date: ______________

Rubric 3
Scoring Rubric for Scientific Process

Directions for Use: Score students on the responses to each of the questions.

	Criteria	Strong Evidence 3	Some Evidence 2	Little Evidence 1	No Evidence 0
1	**Generates a Prediction**	Clearly generates a prediction appropriate to the experiment.	Somewhat generates a prediction appropriate to the experiment.	Generates an inappropriate prediction.	Fails to generate a prediction.
2	**Lists Materials Needed**	Provides an inclusive and appropriate list of materials.	Provides a partial list of materials needed.	Provides inappropriate materials.	Fails to provide a list of materials needed.
3	**Lists Experiment's Steps**	Clearly and concisely lists four or more steps as appropriate for the experiment design.	Clearly and concisely lists one to three steps as appropriate for the experiment design.	Generates inappropriate steps.	Fails to generate steps.
4	**Arranges Steps in Sequential Order**	Lists steps in sequential order.	Lists most of the steps or one step out of order.	Lists one or two steps or steps are placed in an illogical order.	Does not list steps.
5	**Plans Data Collection**	Clearly states a plan for data collection, including what data will be needed and how they will be recorded.	States a partial plan for data collection, citing some items for collection and some way of recording data.	Provides a minimal plan for either data collection and/or recording.	Fails to identify any part of a plan for data collection.
6	**States Plan for Interpreting Data for Making Predictions**	Clearly states a plan for interpreting data by linking data to prediction.	States a partial plan for interpreting data that links data to prediction.	Provides a brief statement that partially addresses use of data for prediction.	Fails to state a plan for using data for making a prediction.

Total points possible: 18

Note. Adapted from Fowler (1990).

Lesson 2: What Is a Scientist?

Planning the Lesson

Instructional Purpose

- To learn the characteristics of scientists and the investigation skills that scientists use.

Instructional Time

- 45 minutes

Scientific Investigation Skills and Processes

- Make observations.
- Ask questions.
- Learn more.
- Design and conduct experiments.
- Create meaning.
- Tell others what was found.

Assessment "Look Fors"

- Students can distinguish between scientists and nonscientists.
- Students should be able to identify the scientific investigation processes used by scientists.

Materials/Resources/Equipment

- Lab coat for teacher
- One lab coat (white adult T-shirt or dress shirt) for each student
- Beaker
- Microscope
- Prepared PowerPoint slides or transparencies of Handout 2A (Blank Frayer Model of Vocabulary Development on Scientists) and Handout 2B (Completed Frayer Model of Vocabulary Development on Scientists)
- One copy of Handout 2B (Completed Frayer Model of Vocabulary Development on Scientists) for each group of three or four students
- Markers or pens
- One piece of chart paper
- Student log books
- Blank nametags

Implementing the Lesson

1. Put on a lab coat and pick up a beaker and microscope. Ask the students what kind of job you might have. Explain that you are a scientist. Ask the students if they know a scientist and allow them to discuss what they know about scientists or their experiences with scientists. Record student responses to the following questions:
    - Do you know a scientist?
    - What do you think scientists do?

DOI: 10.4324/9781003238775-10

- Name a few famous scientists and discuss their contributions (e. g., Edison—filament).

2. Display the Completed Frayer Model of Vocabulary Development on Scientists (Handout 2B). Cover entries in each section with sticky notes so students cannot read them until the appropriate time. Ask the students what they think scientists do. Write down their definition on the board.
3. Uncover the definition section of the Frayer graphic to reveal the following definition of a scientist: "a person who studies nature and the physical world by testing, experimenting, and measuring" (Scholastic, 1996). Ask students:
   - How is the class' definition of a scientist like (or different from) this definition?

4. Divide the class into small groups of three or four students. Explain and assign roles to each student in the group: recorder, reporter, supporter (manages materials, keeps the group on task, and encourages), and timekeeper.
5. Give each group the Blank Frayer Model of Vocabulary Development on Scientists (Handout 2A) on chart paper with the definition in the appropriate section. Ask groups to write down what a scientist does in the appropriate section (scientific investigation processes). Have reporters share group answers with the class.
6. Using Handout 2B, uncover the section titled "What Scientists Do . . . " to show the science process skills. Ask students to compare and contrast this list with what they wrote down. Quickly explain each item listed and add that students will learn more in the science unit to help them:
   - Make observations.
   - Ask questions.
   - Learn more.
   - Design and conduct experiments.
   - Create meaning.
   - Tell others what was found.

7. Explain that there are many different types of scientists. A geologist is an example of a person who studies the Earth, soil and rock formations, mineral fossils, and natural resources. Have groups write down types of scientists. Share responses with the class and then compare and contrast these responses with the types listed on the large group chart. Note that each word ends with the suffix "-ist" and that this suffix means "a person who."
8. Repeat the process described above for #7 and ask students to give nonexamples of scientists and then share their responses. Lead students in a discussion about whether anyone can be a scientist, using the following prompts:
   - Explain whether you think everyone is a scientist.
   - What makes someone a scientist?
   - When is someone *not* a scientist?

9. Explain to the students that they are going to learn how to think like a scientist and learn how to do what scientists do. Show students the book *What Is a Scientist?* by Barbara Lehn. Tell students to look for the scientific investigation processes while you are reading the book to them. Refer to the "What Scientists Do . . . " list and discuss the following after reading the book:
   - What scientific investigation skills did we read about in the book?
   - What scientific investigation processes do you use? When do you use them?

- What is something you would like to investigate?

10. Have students put on their "lab coats" and nametags with "Professor (child's name)." Tell them to get used to feeling like a scientist because during Lesson 3 they are going to be engaging in the scientific investigation process.
11. Have students take out their student logs and respond to the prompt, "To think like a scientist means I will . . ." If time allows, have students share their responses.

Concluding and Extending the Lesson

Concluding Questions and/or Actions

- Describe how scientists study change.
- Describe whether you would or would not like to be a scientist.

What to Do at Home

- Tell students to ask their parent or some other adult to respond to the question, "What would you investigate/study/do if you were a scientist?"

Name:______________________________ Date: ________________

Handout 2A
Blank Frayer Model of Vocabulary Development on Scientists

Definition	What Scientists Do . . . (Scientific Investigation Processes)
Scientists	
Examples	Nonexamples

Name:______________________________ Date: _______________

Handout 2B
Completed Frayer Model of Vocabulary Development on Scientists

Scientists

Definition	What Scientists Do . . . (Scientific Investigation Processes)
"a person who studies nature and the physical world by testing, experimenting, and measuring"	• Make observations. • Ask questions. • Learn more. • Design and conduct experiments. • Create meaning from experiments. • Tell others what was found.
Examples	**Nonexamples**
• Astronomers—study the universe (planets, stars, etc.) • Biologists—study living plants and animals • Geologists—study the Earth's layers of soil and rocks (sediments and mineral fossils) • Physicists—study matter and energy	• Entertainers • Poets • Bankers

Lesson 3: The Concept of Change

Planning the Lesson

Instructional Purpose

- To understand the concept of change and develop generalizations about the concept of change.

Instructional Time

- 45 minutes

Change Concept Generalizations

- Change is everywhere.
- Change is related to time.
- Change can be natural or manmade.
- Change can be random or predictable.

Assessment "Look Fors"

- Students can brainstorm things that change and classify them into categories.
- Students can provide examples of each of the change generalizations.
- Students can apply the change generalizations to the clay and oil experiment.

Materials/Resources/Equipment

- Chart paper for each group of four students
- Handout 3A (Taba Concept Model for Change) for students to complete
- One pack of sticky notes per group of three to four students
- Markers
- Four sentence strips with a different change generalization written on each strip
- Student logs, one for each student
- A large class poster of Handout 3A if the handout cannot be projected
- Examples of erosion and weathering, using either physical objects or photographs. Images should include examples students will be familiar with, such as images from the local area or other well-known places. Examples can be found at:
  - http://science.nationalgeographic.com/science/photos/weathering-erosion-gallery
  - http://www.pbslearningmedia.org/asset/ess05_img_erosion

- Story about the collapse of Utah's "Wall Arch" at Arches National Park with before and after pictures: http://www.nps.gov/arch/parknews/news080808.htm

Implementing the Lesson

1. Tell students they are going to explore a concept that is important to understanding our world: change. Explain that scientists spend a lot of their time trying to explain why a change occurred or to make change occur. Ask:
   - How do scientists study change?

DOI: 10.4324/9781003238775-11

2. Explain that scientists often study change by making observations and that sometimes the observations take place over long periods of time. Show pictures of the Wall Arch at Arches National Park before and after it collapsed on August 4, 2008. Ask students:
   - How do you think the Wall Arch was created?
   - How long do you think it took for the Wall Arch to be formed?
   - Why do you think the Wall Arch collapsed?

3. Use discussion to lead students to understand that the Wall Arch was originally a solid rock. The arch was formed over a very long time through the processes of weathering and erosion that changed the solid rock into an arch. The continued effects of weathering and erosion weakened the arch until it collapsed. The collapse of the arch was a change caused by weathering and erosion.
4. Display Handout 3A (Taba Concept Model for Change).
5. Create small groups of three to four students each. Give each group sticky notes, markers, and a copy of Handout 3A. Tell each group to think of examples of change and to write or draw one idea on each sticky note. Circulate as the groups complete this task, checking for student understanding of the task. Have each group share their examples with the whole class and record examples from each group on the class chart. After each group has shared, they will place their sticky notes on their group's chart section labeled "Examples of Change."
6. Discuss what it means to classify things into categories. Remind students that in order to classify objects, they must find some way in which the objects are similar. Ask students:
   - Can you classify your change examples into categories?

7. Once the students are satisfied with the categories, they will create group categories on the chart and label each category. Each group will share the categories they identified with the whole class and record the categories on the section of the class chart labeled "Categories of Change."
8. In groups, have students brainstorm nonexamples of change. Ask students:
   - What never changes?

9. Have the students write one nonexample per sticky note and each group will share their nonexamples with the class. Nonexamples will then be recorded on the class chart. Ask students: What can you say about change based on the examples and nonexamples?

10. Provide students one example as a model, such as "I notice that there are many different kinds of changes." Have the students record this statement on the section of the chart labeled "Generalizations About Change." Explain that scientists often "generalize" or make statements about what they notice across several examples, observations, or investigations, and those generalizations help scientists to make sense of the world. In order to make generalizations, a scientist must infer how the examples, observations, or investigations are alike. Ask students:
    - Pretend that you are scientists and create one "generalization" that you know about change.
    - Record that generalization on your group chart.

11. Circulate around the room as students work to create their generalizations. Ask groups to share their generalizations. Generalizations should include:
    - Change is everywhere.
    - Change is related to time.
    - Change can be natural or manmade.
    - Change can be random or predictable.

12. Post the chart of generalizations about change in the classroom and tell students you will be discussing changes in their world throughout the next few weeks. Ask students the following question and have them defend their answers:
    - Think about the pictures of the Wall Arch that you saw at the beginning of the lesson. Which change generalizations might scientists use to describe the changes to the Wall Arch?

13. Make sure students explain changes that happened to the Wall Arch using the change generalizations. Ask students:
    - How did the Wall Arch show changes over time?
    - Do you think the changes in the Wall Arch were random or predictable? Why?
    - What are some of the natural changes that occurred? Manmade changes?

14. Have students take out their logs and choose two of the following questions:
    - How do you think scientists study change?
    - Why is the concept of change useful when observing the Wall Arch?
    - Are there other ways to investigate change in our world?
    - What does a scientist have to do in order to make a generalization?
    - Do you think that a generalization is always true? Why or why not?

Concluding and Extending the Lesson

What to Do at Home

- Identify examples of change you see at home and list the change generalization that relates to that example of change. Be prepared to share your findings with your classmates in the next session.

Name:____ Date: __________________

Handout 3A
Taba Concept Model for Change

Examples of Change	Categories of Change
Nonexamples of Change	**Generalizations About Change**

Lesson 4: Becoming a Geologist

Planning the Lesson

Instructional Purposes

- To explore the characteristics of a particular type of scientist: a geologist.
- To define geology.

Instructional Time

- 45 minutes

Key Science Concepts

- The Earth's surface changes continuously over time.
- Geologists study changes in the Earth.

Scientific Investigation Skills and Processes

- Ask questions.

Assessment "Look Fors"

- Students can ask questions pertaining to the work of geologists.
- Students can find resources about the work of geologists.
- Students can understand and describe the role of geologists.

Materials/Resources/Equipment

- Projector and screen
- Online access to http://kids.earth.nasa.gov/archive/career/geologist.html and http://www.agiweb.org/workforce/brochure.html
- (Optional) "So You Want to be a Geologist," a 2-minute video from Adventures in Education that explains what geologists do: http://www.youtube.com/watch?v=XVfkP0kuyog&feature=youtu.be
- (Optional) "Careers in Geology," an episode of the television program *On the Job* that highlights careers in geology, courtesy of the University of Alabama: http://www.youtube.com/watch?v=UZR8MiTJDA0&feature=youtu.be
- (Optional) "Why I Became a Geologist," a one-minute video from the Environmental Science Institute in which Dr. Randy Marett explains why he became a geologist: http://www.youtube.com/watch?v=Feq5pwH2TFw&feature=youtu.be
- Markers or pens
- Student logs
- Handout 4A (Blank Frayer Model of Vocabulary Development: Geologists) for each group of three to four students
- Copy of Handout 4B (Completed Frayer Model of Vocabulary Development: Geologists) to project onscreen

Implementing the Lesson

1. Display pictures of equipment used by geoscientists (or bring examples of equipment) at the front of the room. Tools can include a rock pick, compass, altimeter, binoculars, etc. Ask students:

DOI: 10.4324/9781003238775-12

- What kind of scientist uses the equipment on display?
- What is geology?
- What does a geologist do?

2. Allow them to discuss what they know about geology or their experiences with geologists. Or, show a video clip that highlights what geology is and what geologists do. Review the definition of geology—the study of the solid earth, its rocks and minerals—with students.
3. Display Handout 4B (Completed Frayer Model of Vocabulary Development: Geologists) on a projector or screen. Cover entries in each section with sticky notes so students cannot read the answers until the appropriate time. Ask students:
   - How would you define "geologist"?

4. Record the definition. Reveal the definition section of the Frayer Model: "Geologists are scientists who work to understand natural processes on Earth by studying the materials, processes, products, physical nature, and history of the Earth." Ask students:
   - How is your group's definition of geologist like (or different from) this definition?

5. Divide the class into small groups of three to four students. Give each group Handout 4A (Blank Frayer Model of Vocabulary Development: Geologists) on chart paper with the definition in the appropriate section. Ask students:
   - What do geologists do?

6. Remind students that the video clip shown earlier in the lesson provided several examples of what geologists do. Have students record what a geologist does in the appropriate section of Handout 4A. Have the groups choose one member to be their reporter who shares their responses with the class.
7. Uncover the section titled "What Geologists Do" to show what geologists' jobs involve. Geologists work in the field, the laboratory, and the office. Field work consists of making observations, exploring the surface using tools, collecting samples, and making measurements to analyze in the laboratory. Geologists may also conduct experiments or use computer models to test their theories about geologic processes. At the office, geologists create reports using the data they have collected and the results of the analyses they conducted. Discuss how geologists use science process skills in their work such as:
   - Make observations.
   - Ask questions.
   - Learn more.
   - Design and conduct experiments.
   - Create meaning from observations.
   - Tell others what was found.

8. Explain that there are many different types of geoscientists. Show students the list of geosciences on http://www.agiweb.org/workforce/brochure.html, or review the different types of geologists that were discussed in the video clip. Then, have the class complete the examples section on Handout 4A. Ask students:

- Can you think of some nonexamples of geologists? Have groups record their nonexamples of geologists and share responses with the class.
- Can everyone be a geologist? Explain.
- What makes a geologist a geologist?
- When is a scientist NOT a geologist?

9. Ask students:
   - What examples of the scientific investigation process were discussed in the video clip or on the website? Have students discuss the examples.

10. Ask students:
    - What scientific investigation skills did we hear about?
    - What scientific investigation processes do you use? When do you use them?
    - What is something you would like to investigate?

11. Have students take out their student logs and respond to the statement "To think like a geologist means I will . . . " Provide time for students to write and allow time for students to share their responses with a partner.

Concluding and Extending the Lesson

What to Do at Home

- Have students ask a parent or some other adult to respond to the question, "What would you do to think like a geologist?" or "What would you investigate if you were a geologist and how would you investigate it?" Allow time before the next lesson for students to share their responses with the class.

Name:__________________________________ Date: ________________

Handout 4A
Blank Frayer Model of Vocabulary Development: Geologists

Definition	What Geologists Do

Geologists

Examples	Nonexamples

Name:______________________________________ Date: __________________

Handout 4B
Completed Frayer Model of Vocabulary Development: Geologists

Geologists

Definition

"Geologists are scientists who work to understand natural processes on Earth by studying the materials, processes, products, physical nature, and history of the Earth."

What Geologists Do

- Collect specimens
- Make measurements
- Work in the field, the lab, and the office
- Analyze samples
- Create reports
- Use technology such as GPS
- Find resources
- Make predictions

Examples

- Engineering geologists
- Paleontologists
- Volcanologists
- Marine geologists

Nonexamples

- Botanist (studies plants)
- Meteorologist (studies weather)
- Microbiologist (studies microscopic organisms)

Lesson 5: Rock Detectives

Planning the Lesson

Instructional Purpose

- To apply the steps of the Wheel of Scientific Investigation and Reasoning.

Instructional Time

- 60 minutes

Key Science Concepts

- There are three types of rock: igneous, metamorphic, and sedimentary.
- Rocks are made up of minerals.
- Rocks change due to various processes and influences such as weathering, erosion, heat, pressure, and layering (rock cycle).

Scientific Investigation Skills and Processes

- Make observations.
- Ask questions.
- Learn more.

Assessment "Look Fors"

- Students can identify and describe the three types of rocks.
- Students can describe how each type of rock is formed.
- Students can understand that rocks are made of minerals.
- Students can describe the ways that rocks change due to various processes such as weathering, erosion, heat, pressure, and layering (rock cycle).

Materials/Resources/Equipment

- Handout 5A (Wheel of Scientific Investigation and Reasoning)
- Computer with access to Internet
- Projector and screen
- Markers or pens for students
- Student logs
- Samples of rocks (one type per group):
    - Set A: obsidian, basalt, and granite (igneous)
    - Set B: limestone, shale, coal, and sandstone (sedimentary)
    - Set C: quartzite, slate, marble, and gneiss (metamorphic)

- Magnifying glasses (one per student, if possible)
- Crayons and colored pencils
- Handout 5B (Comparing Rocks)
- Handout 5C (Blank Rock Concept Map)
- Handout 5D (Completed Rock Concept Map)

Implementing the Lesson

1. Explain to students that they are going to learn to "think like a scientist" and apply science processes.

DOI: 10.4324/9781003238775-13

2. Have students share their student log responses, as well as their family members' responses, to the prompt: "To think like a scientist, I will . . ."
3. Review what students have learned about scientists from Lesson 4 about what geologists do. Tell students that they will be learning more about what geologists do.
4. Distribute copies of Handout 5A (Wheel of Scientific Investigation and Reasoning) to all students and discuss the six components. Have students glue Handout 5A into their student logs and date the entry. Using the following questions, prompt students to see the relationship between the scientific investigation processes that were discussed during the previous class period and the components included on the wheel. Ask students:
   - What do you notice about the Wheel of Scientific Investigation and Reasoning?
   - What processes do you think that scientists use BEFORE they conduct an experiment?
   - What do scientists do to conduct an experiment?
   - What do scientists do AFTER they conduct an experiment?
   - Which part of an investigation do you think would be most difficult? Why?

5. Tell students that they are going to work like scientists and conduct a scientific investigation. Divide students into three groups and distribute sets of rocks, magnifying glasses, and coloring equipment to the groups.
6. Explain to students that sometimes scientists use charts to record observations. They will use a chart, Handout 5B (Comparing Rocks), to record their initial observations. Model how to use the chart. Direct students' attention to the first section of the Scientific Wheel: Make Observations. Ask students:
   - What do you notice about your rocks?
   - What are the similarities and differences between your rocks?
   - What colors, size, texture, and shape are your rocks?

7. Have students use a magnifying glass to look closely at the rocks. Students should record observations on the chart and use crayons or colored pencils to draw pictures of the rocks. After students are done with the first set of rocks, have them rotate through stations to examine the other two sets of rocks. Allow students to share their observations with the group. Ask students:
   - Compare and contrast the different rocks. What differences do you observe?
   - What do you think caused the differences?

8. Direct students' attention to the second section of Handout 5A labeled "Ask Questions." Model this section by showing students one question you have written on a sentence strip. Ask students:
   - Do you have other questions about the rocks? Have students record their questions on chart paper.

9. Refer to the third step on Handout 5A: "Learn More." Ask students:
   - How can you learn more about something?
   - What do you think is the best way to learn about these rocks? Why?

10. Share with the students that rocks are made up of minerals and that geologists classify rocks into three categories:
    - Igneous: rocks that were created by intense heat, such as when molten magma cools.
    - Sedimentary: rocks that formed when sand, mud, and pebbles were deposited by water, air, or ice. Over time, they were pressed together and cemented.
    - Metamorphic: rocks that went through a change in structure, composition, or texture due to pressure and heat.

11. Tell students that they are going to classify the rocks as geologists would. Ask students:
    - Which of the groups of rocks (A, B, and C) belongs to each category?
    - Which group of rocks looks like it may have been melted? How can you tell?
    - Which group of rocks looks like it was formed by sand, mud, and pebbles that were deposited? How can you tell?
    - Which group of rocks looks like it may have been squeezed and heated, but not to the point of melting? How can you tell?
    - Can you identify two different rocks that illustrate a change from one category of rock to another? For example, could one of these rocks be changed into another by squeezing and heating? Explain your answer.

12. Visit the rock database at http://archive.fossweb.com/modules3-6/EarthMaterials/activities/rockdatabase/index.html to show students additional examples of each rock type. Then lead students in creating a concept map of rock classifications in Handout 5C (Blank Rock Concept Map).
13. Distribute Handout 5D (Completed Rock Concept Map) and have students compare their own rock concept maps from Handout 5C with it.
14. Have students respond to the following prompt: *When observing the rocks, I found out that....*

Concluding and Extending the Lesson

Concluding Questions and/or Actions

- Students can create a short picture book about the rocks they observed including how they are made and how they can change.
- Students can investigate ways that rocks change from one form to another using the rock cycle. A useful diagram of the rock cycle with animations that show how rocks change can be found at http://www.learner.org/interactives/rockcycle/diagram.html.

What to Do at Home

- Have students work with their family members to learn more about rocks using resources such as books, encyclopedias, or the Internet. Tell students to be prepared to share ONE fact about rocks with their classmates.

Name:______________________________ Date:______________

Handout 5A
Wheel of Scientific Investigation and Reasoning

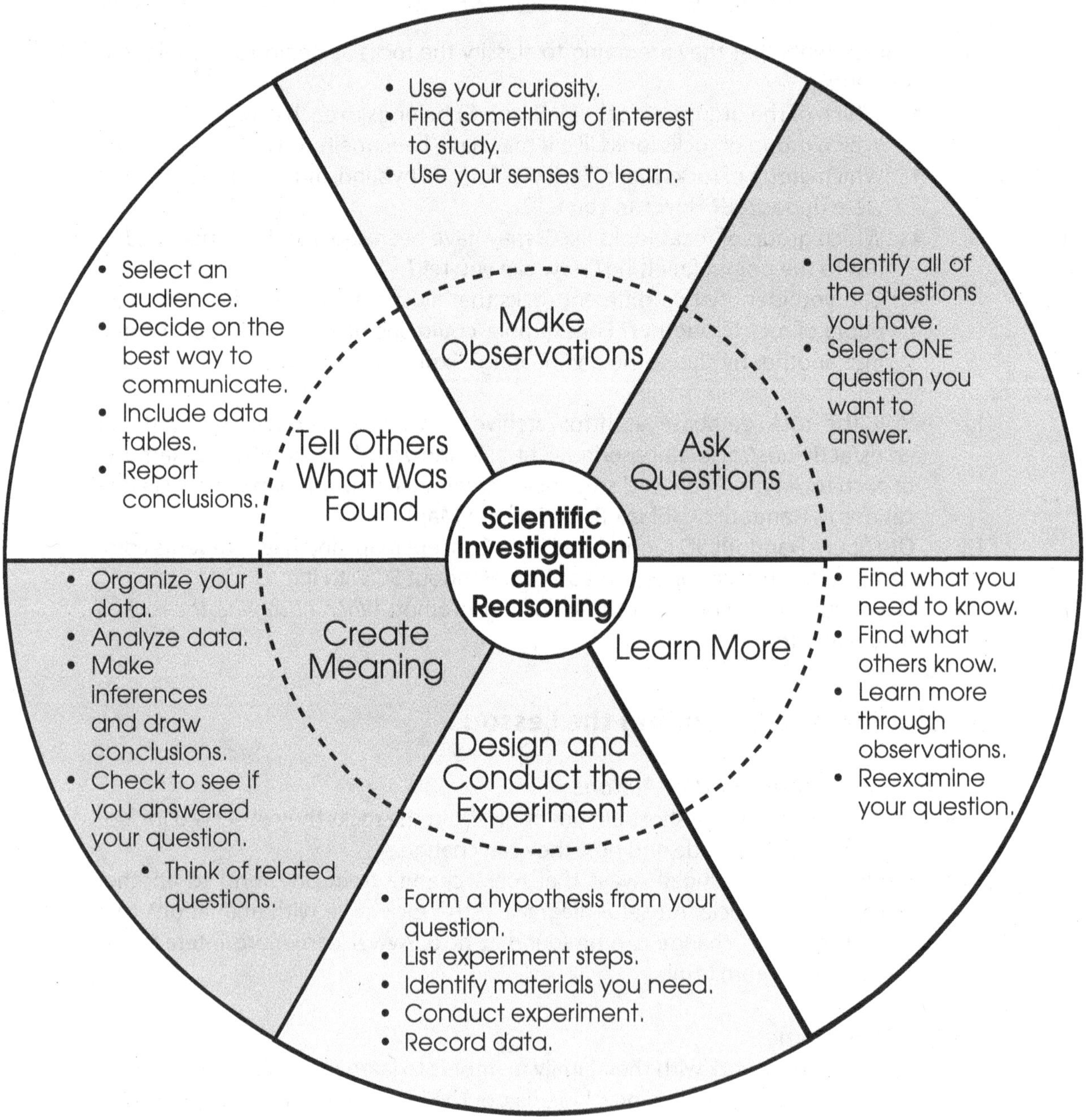

Name:____ Date: ____________________

Handout 5B
Comparing Rocks

Directions: List the attributes of the rocks including: colors, texture, shape, and size. Then draw pictures of two rocks from each set.

Rock Set
Rock Set A:
Rock Set B:
Rock Set C:

Name:______________________________ Date: ______________

Handout 5C
Blank Rock Concept Map

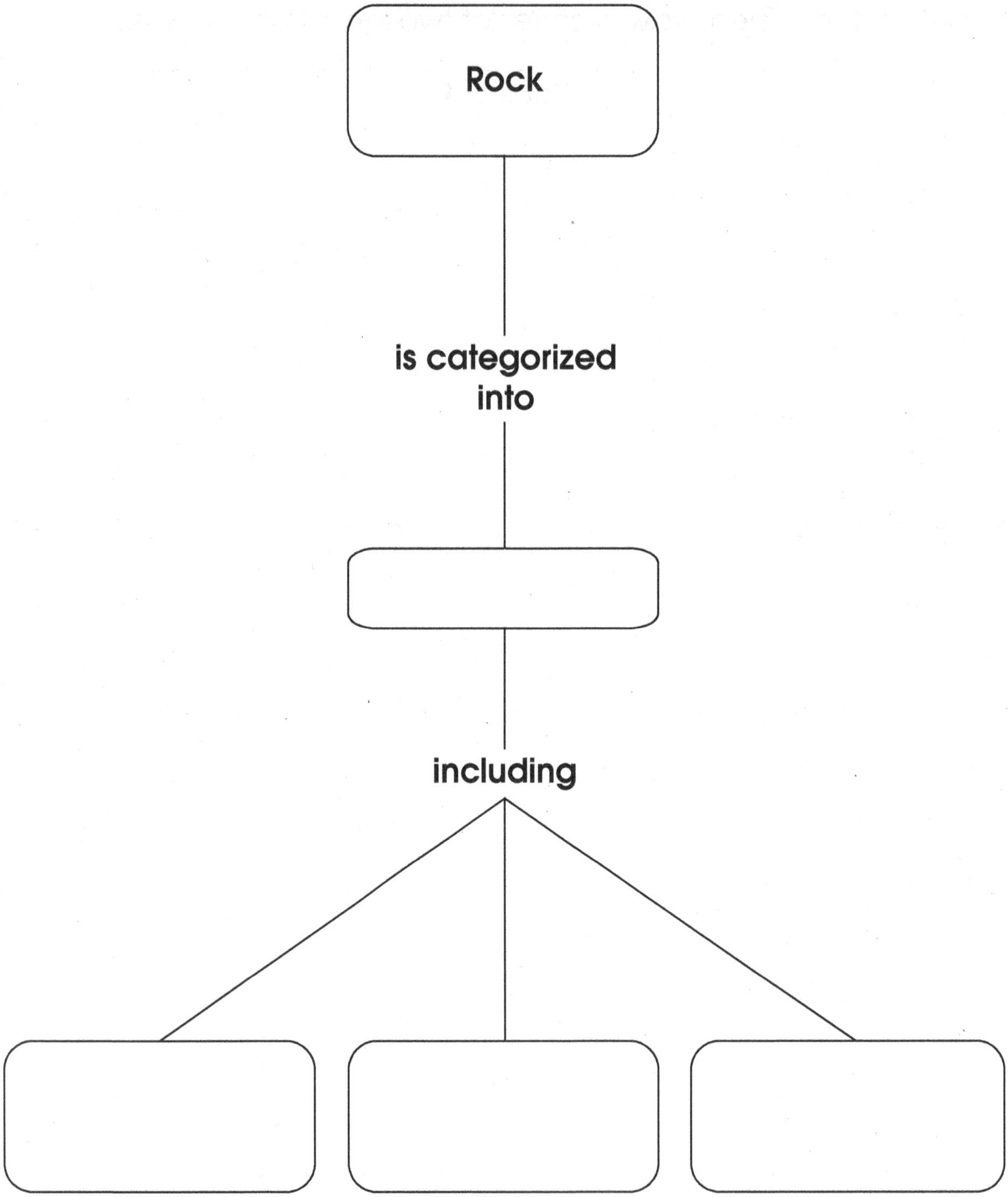

Name:______________________________ Date: ______________

Handout 5D
Completed Rock Concept Map

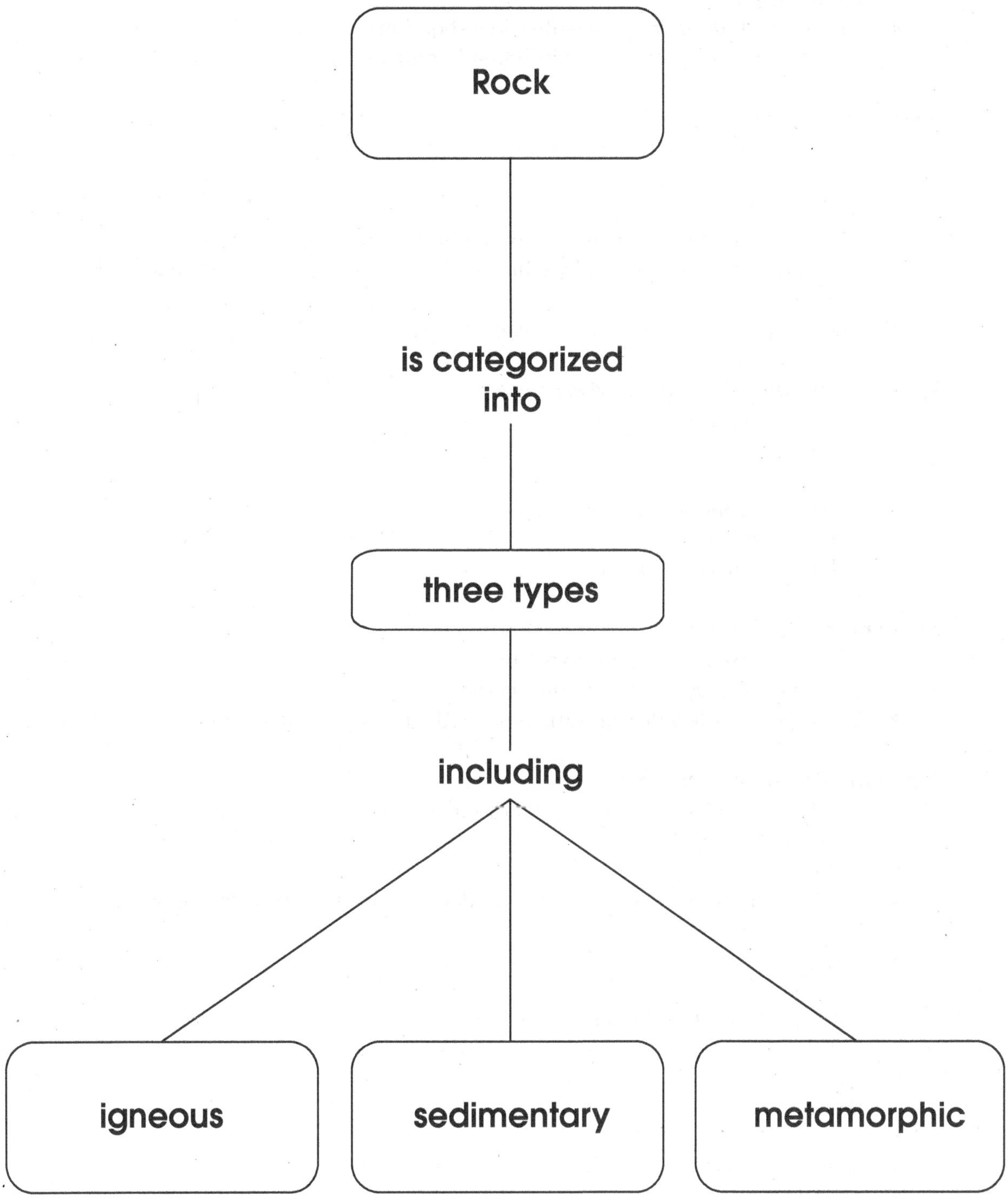

Lesson 6: Changing Rocks

Planning the Lesson

Instructional Purpose

- To engage students in the scientific investigation process.
- To conduct experiments to explore weathering and erosion.

Instructional Time

- Two class periods of 45 minutes each

Key Science Concepts

- Weathering is the mechanical and chemical process that decomposes rock, while erosion is the process by which those rock particles are carried away by wind or water.
- One component of soil is small pieces of rock.

Scientific Investigation Skills and Processes

- Make observations.
- Ask questions.
- Learn more.
- Design and conduct experiments.
- Create meaning.
- Tell others what was found.

Assessment "Look Fors"

- Students make detailed observations.
- Students correctly respond to questions.
- Students accurately describe and analyze the process of weathering.

Materials/Resources/Equipment

- Handouts 6A–6E (Weathering and Erosion Handout Set)
- Collection of rocks
- Sugar cubes
- Books about rocks and minerals (see Student Resources on p. 11 for suggestions)
- Plastic fillable eggs
- Pieces of chalk
- Vinegar
- Small plastic bottle with cap
- Rocks
- Water
- Wood
- Freezer
- Safety Goggles (for Station 5)
- Jars labeled A and B
- Steel file
- Pieces of limestone or hard candies
- Sandpaper (fine, medium, rough)
- Newspaper or disposable table cloth

DOI: 10.4324/9781003238775-14

- Sponge
- Student logs

Implementing the Lesson

1. Show students the collection of rocks that includes various sizes, shapes, and textures. Distribute rocks to each student. Ask students:
   - How is the rock similar to and different from other rocks?
   - How can rocks change? Guide students to the understanding that the rocks were once part of larger rocks.
   - When rocks break apart, are the edges likely to be smooth or rough? Show students a rock that has been broken.
   - Think of rocks that you may have found along a river or at the beach. Describe the rock that you found and provide a reason for why the rocks found there are smoother.
   - Talk with a partner about ways that rocks can become smaller and smoother. Did these changes occur in nature or were they caused by man?

2. Tell students that there is one process that breaks rocks down into smaller pieces called weathering and a second process called erosion that carries the broken pieces away. Ask students:
   - How do weathering and erosion happen?

3. Tell students that in this lesson they are going to focus on the subjects of weathering and erosion. Let students know that they will be working like scientists, asking questions, gathering information, experimenting, recording data, and drawing conclusions. Have students work in pairs and complete three of the weathering lab activities. Explain that scientists perform repeated trials in their experiments to see if the results are the same or different. Explain that they will be participating in multiple activities, and their results will be compared in a discussion the following day.
4. Introduce the Lab Stations to the students and direct them to glue each activity handout (Handouts 6A–6E) into their student logs. Tell students that after performing the experiment, they should clean their station and rotate to their next activity. A signal, such as ringing a bell, may be used to let students know when to move to the next activity.

Lab Stations:

Station #1: Freezing

Materials: bowl, plate, weight

This station is designed to show students that moisture flows into the small cracks in rocks, expands when it freezes, and breaks rocks. This activity will take place over 2 days. On the first day, fill a bowl to the rim with water and place the plate and weight on top. Students should observe this procedure. The plate should be touching the surface of the water. Place it in the freezer overnight. On the second day, remove the bowl and have students examine it. Students should notice that the ice lifted the plate and weight because the water expanded as it froze. Water is a powerful weathering factor when combined with freezing temperatures.

Station #2: Moving Water

Materials: Two jars (labeled A and B), hard candy, water, 1-cup liquid measuring cup

Have students pour 1 cup of water into each jar and then drop a piece of candy into each jar. Have students cover both jars. Have students shake Jar A, but they should not disturb Jar B. Students should notice that the disturbed candy has dissolved much more than the undisturbed one.

Station #3: Wind

Materials: Plastic eggs and sugar cubes

Give each student a plastic egg and a sugar cube. Have the students place the sugar cube inside the egg and then shake the egg vigorously. The movement of the sugar cube inside the egg signifies wind blowing smaller rocks against larger rocks.

Station #4: Acid

Materials: chalk (limestone), vinegar, plastic container

Have students fill the plastic container with vinegar and drop a piece of chalk into the vinegar. The vinegar will dissolve the chalk and provides an example of chemical weathering.

Station #5: Friction

Materials: two different types of rocks, wood, sandpaper, steel file, newspaper or tablecloth, safety goggles

Students will compare and contrast the results of sanding wood and sanding rocks.

1. Direct students to complete the experiments and record results in their student logs. Circulate and assist groups as needed. This lesson will take 2 days; have students review their hypotheses and procedures from the first day when drawing conclusions. Next, have students meet in groups to compare the results of each of their experiments.
2. Finally, have students discuss their results with the class. Be sure to confirm student understanding of the differences between weathering (physical and chemical) and erosion. Weathering is the breakdown of the rock, and erosion is when the pieces are carried away. Ask students:
   - How do weathering and erosion change rock?

Concluding Extending the Lesson

What to Do at Home

- Encourage students to share the results of their science experiments with their family members. Have students look for examples of weathering and erosion outside of the classroom. Students should take, draw, or find pictures that illustrate weathering and erosion and bring them to class.

Name:____ Date: ____________________

Handout 6A
Station #1: Freezing

This experiment involves (check one):

- ☐ a physical change
- ☐ a chemical change
- ☐ erosion

Question: What happens when water freezes overnight?
Hypothesis: I think that . . .

Materials: bowl, plate, water, weight

Steps in Experiment

1. Fill the bowl with water and place a plate on top of the water, touching the surface of the water. Place a weight on top of the plate.
2. Freeze the bowl overnight.
3. Remove the bowl from the freezer and observe what happened.

Data Collection
Observe and record observations. What changed? What happened to the water? What happened to the bowl, plate, and weight?

Analysis
I think this happened because . . .

Was your hypothesis correct? _______

Conclusion
How do these results apply to rocks?

Name:______________________________ Date: ______________

Handout 6B
Station #2: Water

This experiment involves (check one):

- ☐ a physical change
- ☐ a chemical change
- ☐ erosion

Question: What happens when rock (candy) is tumbled over and over?
Hypothesis: I think that . . .

Materials: pieces of limestone or hard candy, two jars with lids labeled A and B, water

Steps in Experiment

1. Pour 1 cup of water into each container.
2. Drop a piece of limestone or hard candy into each container.
3. Cover with a lids.
4. Leave one jar standing. Shake the other jar.
5. Observe what happens.

Data Collection
Observe: Draw a picture of the contents of each jar below.

Jar A (not shaken) **Jar B (shaken)**

What happened to the candy in each jar? What changed?

Analysis

I think this happened because . . .

Was your hypothesis correct? _______

Conclusion

How do these results apply to rocks?

Name:____ Date: ____________________

Handout 6C
Station #3: Wind

This experiment involves (check one):

☐ a physical change
☐ a chemical change
☐ erosion

Question: Will rocks change due to wind?
Hypothesis: I think that . . .

Materials: plastic fillable eggs, sugar cubes

Steps in Experiment

1. Place a sugar cube inside the fillable egg and seal.
2. Shake the egg.
3. Open the egg and observe what happened to the sugar.

Data Collection
What changed? What happened to the sugar cube?

Analysis
I think this happened because . . .

Was your hypothesis correct? ________

Conclusion
How do these results apply to rocks?

Name:____ Date: ________________

Handout 6D
Station #4: Acid

This experiment involves (check one):

- ☐ a physical change
- ☐ a chemical change
- ☐ erosion

Question: Will the rock change when it is exposed to a weak acid?
Hypothesis: I think that . . .

Materials: chalk (limestone), vinegar, plastic container

Steps in Experiment

1. Fill the container with vinegar.
2. Add a piece of chalk.
3. Observe what happens.

Data Collection

Observe results and record observations. What changed? What happened to the chalk?

Analysis

I think this happened because . . .

Was your hypothesis correct? _______

Conclusion

How do these results apply to rocks?

Name:______________________________ Date: ______________

Handout 6E
Station #5: Friction

This experiment involves (check one):

- ☐ a physical change
- ☐ a chemical change
- ☐ erosion

Question: Will the rock change when it is sanded or filed?
Hypothesis: I think that . . .

Materials: two different types of rocks and wood, sandpaper (various grains), steel file, tablecloth or newspaper to protect the table

Steps in Experiment

1. Sand a rough end of the wood. Record the results.
2. File the wood with the steel file. Record the results.
3. Repeat the steps with the different rocks. Record the results.

Data Collection
Observe results and record observations in the table below. What changed? What happened to the wood? The rocks?

	Wood	**Rocks**
Sanding		

	Wood	Rocks
Filing		

Analysis

I think this happened because . . .

Was your hypothesis correct? ________

Conclusion

How do these results apply to rocks?

Lesson 7: Soil Formation

Planning the Lesson

Instructional Purpose

- To engage students in the research process by gathering information from a variety of sources.

Instructional Time

- 45 minutes

Key Science Concepts

- The formation of soil is affected by multiple factors.
- One component of soil is small pieces of rock.
- It takes thousands of years for rocks to break down into soil.

Scientific Investigation Skills and Processes

- Ask questions.
- Learn more.
- Tell others what was found.

Assessment "Look Fors"

- Students can list and describe the factors that affect soil formation.

Materials/Resources/Equipment:

- Access to the Internet
- Computer with projector and speakers
- Handout 7A (Soil Formation Factors)
- Handout 7B (CLORPT Table) for each student
- Plastic bags (two per student)
- Student logs

Implementing the Lesson

1. Begin the lesson by showing the Discovery Education United Streaming clip, "Geologist's Notebook: Making a Mud Pie" (11 minutes), which explains the formation of soil through different types of weathering: http://streaming.discoveryeducation.com/.
2. Ask students:
   - Why does the soil in a desert look so different from soil in a forest? Tell students that soils in different places have their own unique properties—color, texture, moisture retention, depth, layers, etc.—and that the nature of these properties is related to factors that influence soil formation.

3. Tell the class that they will be working in groups to learn about the various ways that soil is formed. Divide the class into five groups and provide them with copies of Handout 7A, which contains information on one particular factor for each group that impacts soil formation. The following websites provide relevant information:

DOI: 10.4324/9781003238775-15

- http://www.geography4kids.com/files/land_soil2.html
- http://www.learner.org/courses/essential/earthspace/session1/closer2.html

4. Have each group read about one soil formation factor and develop a creative method of presenting the information to the rest of the class. Some examples of possible presentations of material are a poster/cartoon, a short skit, a poem, or a song.
5. Have each group present their information to the class. Lead the class in creating a list of the factors and have students record the factors in their student logs. Finally, give students a copy of Handout 7B (CLORPT Table) to glue into their logs.
6. Use a computer and projector to share the website http://forces.si.edu/soils/02_03_05.html with students and view the various soil orders that scientists have identified. Next, inform the class that they will be conducting experiments on soil from their area.

Concluding and Extending the Lesson

Concluding Questions and/or Actions

- Encourage students to learn more about soil formation by visiting the exhibitions in the virtual exhibit entitled "Dig It! The Secrets of Soil", available at http://forces.si.edu/soils.
- Have students respond to the following prompt in a discussion or in a persuasive essay: Which generalization about change is most closely related to the process of soil formation? Provide evidence for your claim.

What to Do at Home

- Have students bring in one or two soil samples in sealed plastic bags for the next class. The soil samples should be from a variety of areas (e.g., under a bush, in a field, on a path, near some flowers, on a shore). A good sample is approximately three handfuls. Tell students to make notes about where they found each sample. Ask students:
  - What is each site like (e.g., amount of water and sunlight available)?
  - What plants grow at each site? What type of animals might you find?
  - If possible, students should take a picture of the site where the soil was found and bring the picture to class with the soil sample.

Name:______________________________ Date: ________________

Handout 7A
Soil Formation Factors

Group 1

The **shape of the landscape** affects the creation of soil. That shape is called the **topography**. The sides of the mountains are slopes. When it rains on a slope, there will be drainage called **runoff**. The runoff carries away small rocks and minerals. This runoff winds up in valleys or in the ocean. It slowly builds up, and the small pieces make soil.

Topography: Topography refers to the shape and direction of the land surface and its slope. This factor determines how water will travel across land and affects the amount of erosion by water. Erosion moves soil from higher to lower elevations. Soils tend to be thicker on flat, low-lying land and thinner on steep slopes. South-facing slopes tend to be warmer than slopes that face north because they receive more sunlight. Because of this, soils on south-facing slopes will tend to be more weathered and drier at any given time.

Group 2

There are **climatic effects** that affect the creation of soil. Moisture, rain, and temperature work together to break down rocks. Weathering breaks down the rocks and hard surface. Runoff and erosion carry broken pieces away. When the temperature goes below and above the freezing point of water, it plays a role in weathering. Liquid water seeps into small cracks in rocks and soil. When water freezes, it expands and the rocks pop open with a cracking sound!

Climate: Soil formation processes are directly linked to the climate in which the soil forms. Climate strongly influences the rate of the weathering of rocks and soil. The amount of precipitation in a region controls the amount of water that enters the ground and greatly affects the rates of chemical and physical weathering. Temperature also influences the formation of soil. In warm climates, weathering is more rapid than in cool climates. The combined influence of temperature and precipitation is also significant. For example, if temperatures are cool, the processes of decomposition and weathering are much slower than if temperatures are warm. In the tropics, where it is warm year-round and rainfall is abundant, weathering occurs very rapidly.

Group 3

What is in the soil is dependent on **geologic factors**. The type of soil under your feet is dependent on the type of **bedrock** deep below the surface. Bedrock breaks down and becomes part of the soil.

Parent Material: Parent material is the geologic and organic material from which soil is formed. The kind of soil that forms in a particular location depends largely on the properties of the parent material and how the minerals it contains respond to temperature, pressure, erosion, and weathering. One important kind of parent material is bedrock, which could consist of igneous, sedimentary, or metamorphic rock. Sediment is another kind of parent material, and it can be deposited by water, wind, glaciers, volcanoes, and other means.

Group 4

Chronological factors play an important part in the process. Chronological means that something is related to time. You need time to make soil. Sediment can move around quickly, but it takes a long time to break down bedrock. We cannot sit and watch this process happen. We have to study it over many years. Also, if we pollute our soil, we can't renew it in our lifetime. It takes hundreds to thousands of years to create new topsoil.

Time: Time addresses how long the other factors of soil formation have been at work weathering the parent material. Younger soils tend to be less developed.

Group 5

Soil formation is also affected by **biological factors**. Soil is composed of half minerals/rocks and half air/water. The organic material in the minerals/rocks or the air/water is the most important biological factor. There are tiny living organisms (e.g., bacteria) that break down organic materials. The organic material could be dead plants or dead animals. The organic material in the soil is called humus. There are also roots and tunneling creatures that work like the microbes. They turn the soil around and move it. They churn the pieces of soil.

Organisms: Plants, animals, and other organisms have an effect on soil formation because they bring nutrient-rich organic matter to the soil. Plants affect the amount of organic matter incorporated into the soil. If vegetation is scarce, as it is in the desert, there will be less organic matter. Animals like insects and earthworms tunnel and burrow in the soil, introducing water and air and bringing subsoil material to the surface and topsoil down below the surface. As earthworms feed, they break down decaying plant matter and eliminate it in their waste, which both enriches the soil and makes it more porous. Microorganisms in the soil help decompose plant and animal remains. Weak acids produced by some microorganisms can even dissolve nutrients in rocks. Certain fungi and bacteria release phosphorous and calcium from minerals in rocks and are important rock-weathering agents.

Name:____________________ Date: __________

Handout 7B
CLORPT Table

CL	O	R	P	T
Climate	**Organisms**	**Relief**	**Parent Material**	**Time**
Temperature affects the rate of chemical reactions that weather rocks and minerals. When there is a lot of rainfall, more minerals are chemically weathered and leave soil layers.	Animals that burrow, spreading plant roots, and enzyme-secreting bacteria and fungi chemically change and physically mix soil.	Topography—the slope and the direction a landscape faces—affects the number of hours of sunlight, temperature, water runoff, erosion, and organic matter buildup.	The chemical makeup of original unweathered rock affects the mineral content of the soil. Parent materials are the underlying bedrock, but can also be sand, silt, or clay that are carried in from somewhere else by wind or water.	Older soils are more weathered than younger soils. In the tropics, soils tend to be old because they have not been affected by the remixing effects of glaciation.

Lesson 8: Components of Soil

Planning the Lesson

Instructional Purpose

- To investigate characteristics of different soils.
- To identify soil layers (horizons).

Instructional Time

- 60 minutes

Key Science Concepts

- Soil provides support and nutrients for plants.
- Rock, clay, silt, sand, and humus are the five components of soil. Rock, clay, silt, and sand come from the weathering of bedrock. Humus comes from the decay of organic material.
- Different mixtures of the five components result in different kinds of soil that are characteristic to a location.

Scientific Investigation Skills and Processes

- Make observations.
- Ask questions.
- Learn more.

Assessment "Look Fors"

- Students can list and describe the components of soil.

Materials/Resources/Equipment

- Students' soil samples
- Plastic plates: one per soil sample
- Newspaper to cover the table
- One small bag, per group, of the following:
    - Sand
    - Clay (can use modeling clay if necessary)
    - Silt (can use chalk dust as substitute if necessary)
    - Rocks and gravel
    - Humus (compost)

- Handout 8A (Comparing Soil Characteristics Chart)
- Magnifying glasses: one for each group if possible
- Latex gloves
- Student logs

Implementing the Lesson

1. Tell students that today they are going to learn about the different components of soil. Lead a discussion of the definitions of these terms related to the understanding of soil: organisms, sediments, weathering, parent material, humus, and soil horizon.

DOI: 10.4324/9781003238775-16

2. Collect the soil samples from the class. Divide the students into groups of four. Give each group two soil samples. Have students lay out newspaper over their tables and pour each soil sample onto a separate plastic plate. Give each pair of students a copy of Handout 8A (Comparing Soil Characteristics Chart) and magnifying glasses for their group members. Encourage students to use their senses to determine the characteristics of each sample. (*Note:* Soil samples should not be directly handled because of the unknown origin of the sample and potential contaminants. Latex gloves should be provided for students to touch the soil.)
3. Have students use Handout 8A to make notes about each sample, using the following procedure:
   - General appearance: What does the soil look like? What size are the grains: large (the particles are readily visible), medium, or tiny? Do you see any stones? These may indicate a sandy or rocky soil. Do you see decaying material, roots, or small animals? These may indicate a fertile soil.
   - Color: Is the soil light, medium, or dark colored? Darker colors may indicate a more fertile soil.
   - Smell: How does the soil smell: no smell, foul, earthy/pine? The amount of humus in a soil affects the smell; a large amount creates an earthy smell.
   - Texture: To investigate the soil's texture, moisten a little bit and rub it between your fingers. Is the soil made up of grains of sand? It will feel rocky and coarse. Does the soil stick together in clumps? A clay soil will feel sticky and plastic. Is the soil made up mostly of dead leaves and other material? A loam soil will feel gritty.

4. Once all groups have recorded their observations, have each student discuss their observations with a student from the other pair in the group of four, comparing and contrasting the two soil samples. Then have students share their observations about the components of the soil to create a class chart. Finally, present the definitions of the components of soil (sand, clay, silt, rocks/gravel, and humus) and have students identify the components that are in their soil samples.
   - **Gravel:** rock fragments that are at least 2 mm in diameter.
   - **Sand:** the largest grains in soil. Sand feels gritty and easily falls through your fingers. When squeezed, sand does not stick together.
   - **Silt:** the medium-sized grains in soil that are larger than clay but smaller than sand. Silt feels smooth and silky to the touch.
   - **Clay:** the smallest soil particles. Clay feels slippery or sticky and breaks into hard clumps if you squeeze it.
   - **Humus:** the organic matter in soil that is usually dark brown or black in color. It contains small bits of rotting material such as leaves, twigs, and living and dead organisms. Humus feels soft when you rub it between your fingers and slightly spongy if you squeeze it.

5. Have students recall the locations that their soil samples came from and match each location with the soil sample that came from that location. Ask students:
   - Were there differences between the soil samples you analyzed?
   - What was different?
   - Why were the samples different?

6. Ask students:
   - How do the different components of soil relate to the concept of change?

7. Lead students to the understanding that all of the inorganic components (gravel, sand, silt, and clay) are the results of the weathering of larger rocks. As the size of the particles get smaller due to continued weathering, the properties of the material change. The organic component, humus, comes from a process of change—the decomposition of plant and animal matter. Therefore, soil results from changes to rock and organic matter.
8. Have students write a short story or create a comic strip about how soil is formed. Ask students:
   - If you were trying to explain how soil is formed and what the components of soil are to a younger sibling, how would you do it? Write a short story or create a comic strip that teaches a young child how soil is formed.

Concluding and Extending the Lesson

Concluding Questions and/or Actions

- Have students create an experiment to find out what type of soil earthworms prefer. For example, students might divide a terrarium into sections and fill each section with a different type of soil, and then place earthworms on the top of the soil. Students should make predictions before the experiment begins. After 24 hours, students can dig up the earthworms and count to see how many worms were in each type of soil.
- Scientists use the Munsell Soil Color Chart to describe soil samples. Students can conduct research to learn about the development and uses for the Munsell Soil Color Chart or, if the resource is available, to identify the colors of their soil samples using the chart.
- Give students a sample of potting soil. Ask students:
  - What are the components of potting soil?
  - Does potting soil include components that are not found in natural soil?
  - What are these components?
  - Why do you think they were added?

What to Do at Home

- Students can make their own humus by collecting leaves, sand, moss, seeds, rotting wood, bits of dead plants, and water. Have students mash and mix all the materials together and compare and contrast their humus with the humus on the ground. Ask students:
  - How is the new humus different from the ground humus in terms of smell, color, and texture?
  - Which generalizations about change can be applied to humus?

Name:______________________________ Date:______________

Handout 8A
Comparing Soil Characteristics Chart

	Appearance	Color	Smell	Texture
_______'s Sample				
_______'s Sample				
_______'s Sample				
_______'s Sample				

Lesson 9: Soil Horizons

Planning the Lesson

Instructional Purpose

- To identify soil layers (horizons).

Instructional Time

- 60 minutes

Key Science Concepts

- There are three layers of soil, or soil horizons: topsoil, subsoil, and bedrock.
- Bedrock is turned into rocks, gravel, sand, silt, and clay through weathering.

Scientific Investigation Skills and Processes

- Make observations.
- Ask questions.
- Learn more.

Assessment "Look Fors"

- Students can describe the soil horizons and how soil horizons are related to the concept of change.

Materials/Resources/Equipment

- Access to Internet
- One small bag, per group, of the following:
  - Sand
  - Clay (can use modeling clay if necessary)
  - Silt (can use chalk dust as substitute if necessary)
  - Rocks and gravel
  - Humus (compost)

- Mason jar: one per group
- Magnifying glasses: one per group, if possible
- Shovel/spade
- White paper: one sheet per group
- Measuring tape: one per group
- White glue: one bottle per group
- Handout 9A (Layers of Soil Diagram)
- Student logs

Implementing the Lesson

1. Tell students that they are going to investigate the soil near the school. After getting permission from the principal, take the class outside to a designated dig spot. The area should be natural (e.g., a bank where the soil has been exposed). Ask students:
   - Is the soil near the surface the same as the soil that is deeper below the surface?

DOI: 10.4324/9781003238775-17

- What do you expect to be different about deeper layers of soil?
- Why would you expect this?

2. Dig a small hole that is 30–60 cm deep. Make one side of the hole perpendicular to the ground and the other side a gradual slope. Scrape the steep side of the cut to ensure a smooth surface. Ask students:
   - How many layers can you see?
   - What colors do you see in each layer?

3. Tell students that these layers are soil horizons. Ask students:
   - How large are the rock particles in each layer?
   - Do you see clay, silt, sand, or gravel?
   - Which layer contains the most humus?
   - Which layer is the oldest?
   - Which layer is the newest?
   - How are the upper layers formed?
   - Are the upper layers related to the deeper layers?

4. Have each group make a permanent record of the soil horizon. Have students crease a sheet of white paper down the center, lengthwise, and run a wide strip of glue along the crease. Have students add soil from each layer to the glue in the same order as the layers in the ground. Let the glue dry and gently shake away any loose soil. When students are finished, fill the hole with soil.
5. Next, return to the classroom and give each group Handout 9A (Layers of Soil Diagram). Tell students they are going to use their samples and observations to create a model of the different layers of soil. Tell students to follow Handout 9A to write or draw the layers of soil in their student logs.
6. Show students the drawing of soil horizons at http://www.enchantedlearning.com/geology/soil. Ask them to identify where the layers of soil begin and end.
7. Lead students in creating a concept map on soil layer classifications. Show them the outlines of the concept map. Encourage students to think back to previous lessons on weathering as well as to think about the exposed soil image from earlier in the lesson. Use the following questions as a guide for completing the concept map activity. Model completion of the concept map as the students work to complete their own. Ask students:
   - What do we know about the soil horizons?
   - What are the different soil horizons?
   - What makes each one different?
   - How are the upper layers related to the deeper layers?
   - How do the layers of soil relate to the concept of change?
   - What changes occurred to create the layers?

Concluding and Extending the Lesson

What to Do at Home

- After getting permission, students can dig a hole in the soil at home. Have students identify the different layers and the different components of the soil. Have students record their observations to include in their student logs and share them with their family members.

Name:______________________________ Date: ______________

Handout 9A
Layers of Soil Diagram

Topsoil: Top layer of soil Mixture of humus, clay, sand, silt, and small rocks Usually very dark brown in color Feels soft and crumbly Contains decaying organic materials such as leaves, twigs, insects, or animals (humus) Usually loosely packed
Subsoil: Middle layer of soil Mixture of clay, sand, silt, and small rocks Usually tightly packed
Bedrock: Bottom layer Solid rock

Lesson 10: Plants and Soil

Planning the Lesson

Instructional Purpose

- To investigate different types of soil and evaluate the effectiveness of each type for supporting plant life.

Instructional Time

- 45 minutes

Key Science Concepts

- Soil provides support and nutrients for plants.
- The composition of the soil affects how well it supports plant life.

Scientific Investigation Skills and Processes

- Make observations.
- Ask questions.
- Learn more.
- Design and conduct experiments.
- Create meaning from experiments.
- Tell others what was found.

Assessment "Look Fors"

- Students can explain how the benefits and drawbacks of each soil type are related to the soil composition.

Materials/Resources/Equipment

- Access to the Internet
- Sample of gravel, clay, sand, silt, and humus per group
- Four wide-mouth jars (one per group)
- Filter paper
- Plastic pitcher of water (one per group)
- Graduated cylinder (one per group)
- 1/4 measuring cup (one per group)
- Potted plant in clear container (for demo)
- Large jar (for demo)
- Small spade
- Student logs

Implementing the Lesson

1. Refer students to Handout 5A (Wheel of Scientific Investigation and Reasoning) in their student logs. Tell students that they are going to conduct investigations that will help them determine which kind of soil would be best for plants. Ask students:
    - What properties of soil are beneficial to plants?
    - Do the properties depend on the type of plant?

DOI: 10.4324/9781003238775-18

- Show students a plant that is potted in a clear container as a visual aid. What does soil provide that plants need to thrive?

2. Guide students to the idea that the soil provides nutrients, physical support, and moisture. Different plants have the same basic needs, but the amounts of each basic need varies with plant type. For example, a cactus needs less moisture than a tomato plant. Therefore, different types of soil will benefit different plants.
3. Divide students into groups of three to four. Have students open their logs to a new page and date it. Give each group samples of rocks/gravel, clay, sand, and humus. Ask students:
   - What is one of the first things a scientist would do?
   - What attributes of the soil components can provide what plants need to thrive?
   - Which soil components can provide what plants need?

4. Direct students to the second section of Handout 5A: "Ask Questions." Ask students:
   - What questions might you ask about the soil and soil components to determine which soil would best support plants? Allow each group to share several of their questions with the class.

5. Direct student attention to the third section of Handout 5A: "Learn More." Ask students:
   - How can you learn more about the topic?
   - Provide students resources to learn more about their question, plants, and soil.

6. Direct student attention to the fourth section of Handout 5A: "Design and Conduct Experiments." Tell students that today they are going to conduct an experiment to answer a question of their choice.
7. Model the process of designing an experiment for the question "Which soil component can hold the most water?" Help students to create a hypothesis. Ask students:
   - How do you think the soil components rank from most to least absorbent?
   - Record student-generated hypotheses on the board.

8. Tell students that scientists design experiments so other scientists can confirm the results. Lead students through the steps of the experiment with the sample of gravel. Tell students that scientists record the steps of their experiment in a log so the procedure may be repeated by other scientists. Use the following steps for the whole-class experiment:
   - Create a cone shape with the filter paper. Do this experiment over a container to catch any water that may spill over.
   - Measure 250 g of gravel and place it in the filter paper cone.
   - Measure 250 ml of water. Record this volume in your log. Slowly pour it evenly over the gravel.
   - Have students make observations of the water that is in the container after passing through the gravel. Ask students:
     - What does the water in the container look like?

- What does the sample look, feel, and smell like after the water was poured?
    - What is the volume of water that passed through the sample?
    - What is the volume of water that was absorbed by the sample? Subtract the volume that passed through from the initial volume to find out how much water was absorbed.

- Repeat this procedure with each of the soil components. Record the data and your observations for each trial.
- Create a bar graph using the class data with the soil component on the x-axis and the volume of water absorbed on the y-axis. This website has an easy-to-use graphing utility: http://nces.ed.gov/nceskids/createagraph has an easy-to-use graphing utility.

9. Have students share their observations with the class. Student observations should include the following:
    - Pouring the water on the rocks/gravel did not change the look, feel, or smell. Most of the water ran through to the container.
    - The clay absorbed most of the water. It became very sticky.
    - The sand let most of the water run through it. When wet, it stuck together, but crumbled easily. The sand feels rough even when wet.
    - The humus absorbed some of the water but also let some water pass through. When wet, it stuck together but pulled apart easily and felt spongy.

10. Ask students to examine the graph of the class data. Ask students:
    - What does the graph tell you about this experiment?
    - What can you infer from this data?

11. Direct students' attention to the fifth section of Handout 5A: "Create Meaning." Instruct students to think about their observations and the class' discussion. Ask students:
    - Why do you think the soil's ability to absorb water is important?
    - Why is knowing which soil component absorbs the most water important?
    - How do the results of this experiment relate to agriculture and geography?
    - What qualities other than absorbency are important for soil to have?

12. Allow students to repeat steps 7–11 to conduct an experiment that attempts to find an answer to a student-generated question about plants and soil. Have students design their own procedure and write the procedure in their logs. Review student procedures before experimentation begins to ensure proper safety precautions are taken. Have students present their procedures, data, analyses, and conclusions to the class on a poster. This activity may take place over several days depending on the hypotheses and methods chosen by students.

Concluding and Extending the Lesson

What to Do at Home

- After getting permission, have students find answers to different student-generated questions about plants and soil. Have each student design his or her own procedure and write the procedure in the student log. Have students share findings with their family members.

Lesson 11: Erosion

Planning the Lesson

Instructional Purpose

- To investigate soil erosion, the negative effects of erosion, and ways to prevent erosion.

Instructional Time

- 60 minutes

Key Science Concepts

- Over time, rocks break down and become part of the soil.
- Topsoil is formed over a long period of time from the weathering of bedrock and subsoil.
- Erosion is when rock, soil, and sediment are carried away. Erosion is caused by wind, water, ice, and gravity.

Scientific Investigation Skills and Processes

- Make observations.
- Ask questions.
- Learn more.
- Design and conduct experiments.
- Create meaning.
- Tell others what was found.

Materials/Resources/Equipment

- Old paint roller trays or 9″ x 13″ baking sheets
- Soil
- Soil with grass growing in it
- Objects to use as barriers to erosion (e.g., compost, mulch, twigs, popsicle sticks, toothpicks)
- Hair dryer
- Water cans filled with water
- Water source
- Student logs

Implementing the Lesson

1. Ask students:
    - What do you know about erosion?
    - What is erosion?
    - What causes erosion?
    - Where do we typically see erosion?

2. Tell students that you will be conducting a demonstration to show how soil is moved and landforms change. The demonstration will show how soil is affected by erosion.

DOI: 10.4324/9781003238775-19

3. Show students a tray of soil. Tell students that the pan of soil used to be covered by plants, but farmers recently harvested the crop. Ask students:
   - How would you describe this soil?

4. Place the soil on a table where everyone can see it. Use a hair dryer to simulate wind blowing over the soil. Tell students to record their observations of the effect of the wind in their student logs. Ask students:
   - What happened to the soil when the wind blew?

5. Tell students that wind is an agent of erosion. Ask students:
   - What might happen if the wind continued to blow?
   - How can we stop or minimize wind erosion?

6. Create a list of student suggestions for minimizing wind erosion on the board or on chart paper. Choose one or two of the student suggestions to test. For example, students may suggest that the soil will not blow away as easily if it is wet. Use water to wet the soil and then simulate the wind to test their prediction. Students may suggest that trees or other plants could be planted to prevent the soil from blowing away. Use a piece of sod to test this prediction.
7. Ask students how human actions contribute to the problem of wind erosion.
8. Tell students that you will now demonstrate water erosion. Show students the second tray of soil and say that it represents a forest where all of the trees were cut down. Water the tray for 1–2 minutes. Allow students to examine the soil in the tray and the runoff collected in the basin. Pour the runoff into a clear jar for closer inspection. Students should see gullies form in the tray and large areas where the soil was washed away. The water in the basin will be muddy and full of sediment.
9. Ask students:
   - What happened when the water ran across the bare soil?
   - Why did this happen?
   - Why is water erosion bad?

10. Explain to students that soil erosion is a serious problem facing farmers throughout the world. Every year billions of tons of topsoil are lost. Discuss why lost topsoil is an issue. Guide students to understand that topsoil is the fertile soil that plants grow in. Tell students it takes 100 years to make one inch of new topsoil. Challenge the students to find ways to reduce the amount of erosion that occurs on sloping farm fields.
11. After the experiment, divide students into small groups and give each group a tray filled with soil. Have students research and discuss possible measures to prevent erosion. Each group will develop a method to decrease erosion and share the method with the class.
12. Divide the students into small groups of two or three students and give each two trays to fill with soil. Students will research and discuss possible options for controlling water erosion on their tray of soil.
13. Provide materials for students to use on their "fields," including compost, various forms of mulch, twigs, popsicle sticks, and toothpicks. Students may use these materials to create terraces, water bars, and roots. Decide on a time limit for research and preparation. This time will vary depending on students' desires to experiment.

14. On the day of the experiment, set up the trays and have students present their methods for erosion control. All groups will be given the same amount of water, pour it from the same height, and tip the trays at the same angle. The class will observe as the rain falls for each group and measure the effects of runoff from each field. Students should note the clarity, color, and amount of runoff from each field.
15. Direct students' attention to the "Create Meaning" section of Handout 5A. Ask students what meaning they can create from this experiment.
16. Lead students to understand that the processes of wind and water erosion in this experiment are the same processes by which the parts of mountains and huge rocks that are broken down by weathering are deposited. Over a very long period of time, bedrock weathers and becomes subsoil. Subsoil continues to weather and combines with decaying organic material to become topsoil.

Concluding and Extending the Lesson

What to Do at Home

- Have students share the results of the experiments they did in class with their family members. They should describe what they think the results show about soil erosion. Have them ask their family members how erosion has been a problem in our world.

Lesson 12: Erosion as Change

Planning the Lesson

Instructional Purpose

- To understand the application of change generalizations to erosion.

Instructional Time

- 45 minutes

Key Science Concepts

- Erosion can be natural or caused by man.
- Erosion is related to the four change generalizations.
- Erosion has positive and negative results.
- Erosion can be fast or slow. The rate of erosion is affected by the topography.

Materials/Resources/Equipment

- Chart paper for each student
- Markers

Implementing the Lesson

1. Ask students:
   - How does erosion relate to the concept of change?
   - Which change generalizations apply?

2. Have students create a picture or diagram that shows the relationship. Have students explain the relationship in paragraph form or orally. Have students do this activity individually.
3. Have students share their diagram in a group of four to five students and explain how erosion is related to the change generalizations.
4. To conclude the lesson, conduct a whole-class discussion of a few of the pictures.
5. Ask students the following questions:
   - How does soil erosion happen? What causes soil erosion?
   - Can soil erosion ever be good? Why or why not?
   - Some soil erosion moves at a slow rate; other examples may be very fast. What influences the rate of erosion?
   - In what kinds of topography would erosion be expected? Where would you not expect erosion?

Concluding and Extending the Lesson

What to Do at Home

- Have students go on an erosion scavenger hunt around their backyards, neighborhoods, nearby forest, or park. They should look for examples of erosion and draw or take a picture of each example. Then, they should classify each example of erosion as natural or caused by man. Have them consider whether steps should be taken to prevent the erosion that was found.

DOI: 10.4324/9781003238775-20

Lesson 13: Erosion Prevention

Planning the Lesson

Instructional Purpose

- To develop students' abilities to research a specific problem

Instructional Time

- Three 45-minute classes

Key Science Concepts

- The rate of erosion depends on multiple factors, including climate-based, geological, and biological factors.
- People can take steps to decrease the rate of erosion that occurs naturally and that is caused by human impact on the land.

Scientific Investigation Skills and Processes

- Make observations.
- Ask questions.
- Learn more.
- Design and conduct an experiment.
- Tell others what was found.

Assessment "Look Fors"

- Students demonstrate understanding of the effects of erosion and the factors that affect the rate of erosion.

Materials/Resources/Equipment

- Handout 13A (Need to Know Board)
- Handout 13B: (Research Model; *Note:* This model is complex and may require multiple lessons to implement. You may want to have students focus on only a few of the model's components.)

Implementing the Lesson

1. Erosion is a major problem that threatens our survival. Discuss why erosion is such a problem when there is soil everywhere. Ask students if the top layer of soil is different from the deeper layers. Students should recall that the topsoil contains humus, which is a nutrient necessary for plant growth. Only this topsoil is good for crop growth. Each year, billions of tons of topsoil are lost to erosion, and replacing one inch of topsoil takes 100 years. Erosion is taken very seriously. Governments spend billions of dollars to teach farmers methods to prevent erosion.
2. Ask students:
   - How can erosion be prevented?

3. As a class, complete Handout 13A (Need to Know Board). Tell students that they will be working in groups of no more than three to research a particular method that could prevent erosion.

DOI: 10.4324/9781003238775-21

4. After students have listed all of their questions about erosion, provide a list of possible research topics and discuss how researching the following topics might address their questions:
    - strip cropping,
    - contour plowing,
    - slash-and-burn tilling,
    - Dust Bowl conditions,
    - terracing,
    - conservation tillage,
    - replanting forests, and
    - sediment fences.

5. Assign students to groups and give each group an issue to explore. Allow students to work with their group to develop a research plan. Have students investigate the issues and develop a list of advantages and disadvantages of each potential solution to erosion.
6. Give each student a copy of Handout 13B (Research Model) and tell students that each member of the group needs to find information, take notes on that information, and report his or her findings to the group.
7. On the first day of this lesson, have students work together to plan their investigations and begin individual research. On the second day, have students share information and develop a presentation to share their findings. The presentation can be an electronic slideshow, a poster, a brochure advertising the product, or another creative product. On the third day, have students present their information about the topic. Lead a class discussion to have the students compare and contrast the methods of erosion prevention, including the positive and negative attributes of each method. Ask students:
    - If you were a landscape engineer, what would you conclude about the most effective approaches to prevent soil erosion? Why?
    - If you were a construction company developing a neighborhood, which methods would you choose? Why?
    - If you were a farmer, which methods would you use? Why?

8. Students will write a short reflection statement about which prevention methods are best for society and why.

Concluding and Extending the Lesson

What to Do at Home

- The students will find out how the land in their area has changed over time. To find out, they can talk to someone who has lived in their area for a long time. The students should ask the interviewee how different the land was when he or she was their age. Were there woods or swamps that no longer exist? If not, what was on the land? The students should summarize what they learned from the interview and present their findings to the class.

Name:______________________________ Date: ______________

Handout 13A
Need to Know Board

What do I know?	What do I need to know?	How will I find out? What resources will I use?	What did I learn?

Name:________________________________ Date:____________

Handout 13B
Research Model

1. Identify your issue or problem.

What is the issue or problem?

Who are the stakeholders and what are their positions?

What is your position on this issue?

2. Read about your issue and identify points of view or arguments through information sources.

What are my print sources?

What are my Internet media sources?

What are my people sources?

What are my preliminary findings based on a review of existing sources?

3. Form a set of questions that can be answered by a specific set of data. Examples:

What would be the results of ________ ?

Who would benefit and by how much?

Who would be harmed and by how much?

My research questions:

4. Gather evidence through research techniques such as surveys, interviews, or analyses of primary and secondary source documents.

What survey questions should I ask?

What interview questions should I ask?

What generalizations do secondary sources give?

What data and evidence can I find in primary sources to support different sides of the issue?

5. Manipulate and transform data so that it can be interpreted.

How can I summarize what I found out?

Should I develop charts, diagrams, or graphs to represent my data?

6. Draw conclusions and make inferences.

What do the data mean? How can I interpret what I found out?

How do the data support my original point of view?

How do they support other points of view?

What conclusions can I make about the issue?

7. Determine implications and consequences.

What are the consequences of following the point of view that I support?

Do I know enough or are there now new questions to be answered?

8. Communicate your findings. (Prepare an oral presentation for classmates based on note cards and a written report.)

What are my purpose, issue, and point of view, and how will I explain them?

What data will I use to support my point of view?

How will I conclude my presentation?

Lesson 14: Contemporary Issue: Fracking

Planning the Lesson

Instructional Purpose

- To determine the potential advantages and disadvantages of hydraulic fracturing (fracking).
- To analyze and evaluate the evidence related to fracking.

Instructional Time

- Three 45-minute classes

Key Science Concepts

- Hydraulic fracturing, or "fracking," is a process by which natural gas and oil are extracted from bedrock by opening and widening fractures below the Earth's surface by injecting a mixture of water, chemicals, and silica sand at high pressure into drilled wells in the Earth (United States Environmental Protection Agency, 2013).
- Recently, modern drilling techniques have made fracking an economical method to harvest natural gas and oil. There are many concerns about the environmental and health risks of fracking.

Scientific Investigation Skills and Processes

- Make observations.
- Ask questions.

Assessment "Look Fors"

- Students demonstrate understanding of the process of hydraulic fracturing (fracking).

Materials/Resources/Equipment

- Video: "Fracking: Positive or Negative Impact?": http://www.pbs.org/newshour/spc/thenews/foreducators/story.php?id=19829&package_id=634
- Internet and print resources about fracking

Implementing the Lesson

1. Show students the video "Fracking: Positive or Negative Impact?" Discuss the definition of fracking with students.
2. Divide students into small groups. Provide each group with Internet and print resources that support one side of the fracking issue. Have each group develop a comprehensive list of reasons supporting their side of the issue.
3. Have students share their information with their classmates in a debate, oral presentation, or other presentation format.

DOI: 10.4324/9781003238775-22

Concluding and Extending the Lesson

What to Do at Home

- The students should look for other articles or videos related to fracking. Have them share their resources with their families.

Lesson 15: Persuasive Writing

Planning the Lesson

Instructional purpose

- To guide students in developing persuasive arguments about erosion.[1]

Instructional Time

- 45 minutes

Key Science Concepts

- Some erosion is preventable.
- There are many prevention methods that can be used to combat erosion, including: strip cropping, contour plowing, terracing, no-till methods, and replanting forests.

Scientific Investigation Skills and Processes

- Create meaning.
- Tell others what was found.

Assessment "Look Fors"

- Students successfully use the Hamburger Model for Persuasive Writing to plan and write an essay.

Materials/Resources/Equipment

- Handout 15A (Hamburger Model for Persuasive Writing)
- Paper and pencils
- Student logs

Implementing the Lesson

1. Topsoil is eroding faster than it forms on much of Earth's farmland. Ask students: Why is it bad to lose topsoil? Guide students to recall that topsoil has the most nutrients and is good for growing crops. If this layer of soil is lost, the amount of crops that can be grown will be reduced. Guide students to also recall that it takes a very long time to make new topsoil.
2. Distribute Handout 15A and have students use the Hamburger Model for Persuasive Writing to develop the introduction, reasons, and conclusion for a short persuasive essay. Provide students with the following prompt: "Our country should research and use methods that prevent erosion of topsoil." Instruct students to decide to either agree or disagree with the statement. Have students use information from the research presentations and from previous experiments to provide three reasons for their opinion and write a conclusion. This is an opportunity to go more in depth and have students do additional research in order to develop arguments on one side of this issue.

---

1 *Note:* In those states which have adopted the Common Core State Standards in English Language Arts, this lesson can be easily adapted to focus on having students write opinion pieces.

DOI: 10.4324/9781003238775-23

Concluding and Extending the Lesson

What to Do at Home

- Students could select the three best persuasive essays written by the class and send them to a local newspaper editor for possible publication.

Name:______________________________ Date: ______________

Handout 15A
Hamburger Model for Persuasive Writing

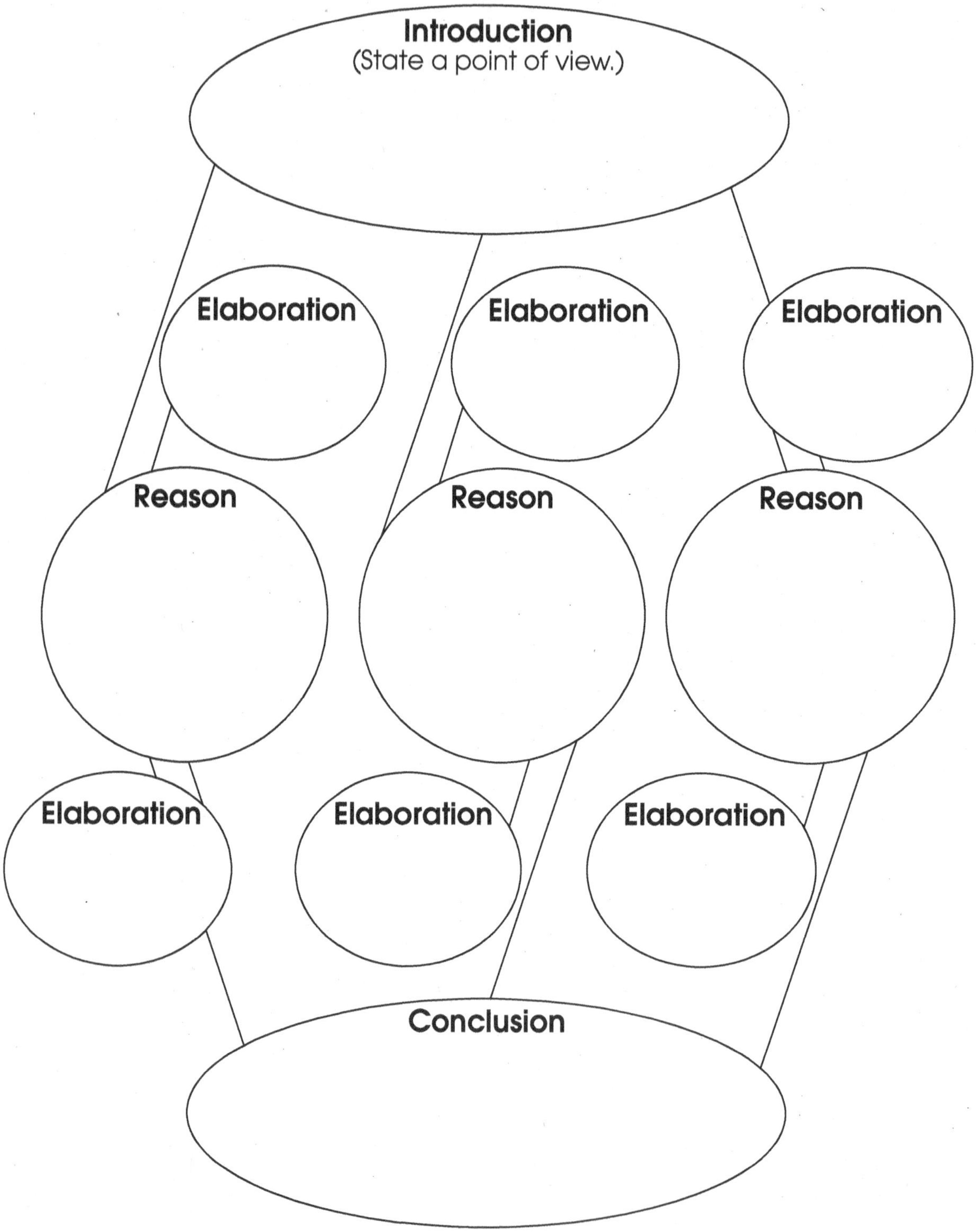

Lesson 16: Putting It All Together

Planning the Lesson

Instructional Purpose

- To review the interrelationships between the concept of change, the scientific process, and unit science content.

Instructional Time

- Two 45-minute periods

Materials/Resources/Equipment

- Chart paper
- Markers

Implementing the Lesson

1. Ask students to complete the following questions in groups of four to five, with one person recording:
   - Content:
     - What new understandings do we have about soil?
     - What do we know about erosion and the impacts of erosion?
     - What have we learned about erosion prevention techniques?
     - Have the questions you asked at the beginning of the unit about scientists' study of rock and soils been answered?

   - Scientific process:
     - What new questions do you have about weathering or erosion?
     - Create a new hypothesis related to one of your questions.
     - List the materials that would be needed to test the hypothesis.
     - List the procedures you would use to test your hypothesis.
     - Describe how you would know if the results of your test supported your hypothesis.

   - Concept of change:
     - Describe how each change generalization is related to the content in this unit.
     - What new generalizations about change can you create based on what you learned in this unit?
     - How is the change related to the scientific process?

2. Ask the groups to share their responses. Discuss similarities and differences between the responses from each group.
3. As a culminating activity, ask students to create a diagram, chart, story, or metaphor that illustrates the most important ideas from this unit of study. Share the results with family members at an open house, on a class website, or in an electronic newsletter.

DOI: 10.4324/9781003238775-24

Concluding and Extending the Lesson

What to Do at Home

- Students could share the diagram, chart, story, or metaphor that illustrates the most important ideas from this unit of study.
- Have students take home their log books and other unit materials. Tell them to share what they have learned with their families.

Lesson 17: Postassessment

Planning the Lesson

Instructional Purpose

- To assess student understanding of the unit macroconcept, student knowledge of the key science concepts in the unit, and student skills in the scientific investigation process.

Instructional Time

- Macroconcept assessment: 30 minutes
- Key science concepts assessment: 30 minutes
- Scientific process assessment: 20 minutes

Materials/Resources/Equipment

- Copies of postassessments for the unit for each student: Handout 17A (Postassessment for Change Concept), Handout 17B: (Concept Map: Soil; this is the postassessment for key science concepts), and Handout 17C (Postassessment for Scientific Process).
- Exemplar Answers for the Postassessment for Change Concept, Exemplar Concept Maps of Soil for Postassessment for Key Science Concepts, and Exemplar Answers for the Postassessment for the Scientific Process
- Pencils

Implementing the Lesson

1. Give each student a copy of the postassessments to complete in the order noted above. The assessments should take no more than 80 minutes in all.
2. Explain that the assessment will be used to see how much students have learned during the unit.

Scoring

- Use the rubrics contained in the preassessment sections for concept, content, and scientific process. Sample exemplar responses are provided after each postassessment.

DOI: 10.4324/9781003238775-25

Name:______________________________________ Date: ____________________

Handout 17A
Postassessment for Change Concept

1. Give as many examples of things that change as you can (up to 10).

______________________ ______________________

______________________ ______________________

______________________ ______________________

______________________ ______________________

______________________ ______________________

2. Draw one example of something that changes, showing before and after the change. Provide as many details as you can.

Before	**After**

3. Identify five ways that a tree could change or be changed.

____

____

____

____

____

4. What are three things you can say about *all* change?

All change __________________________

____

All change __________________________

____

All change __________________________

____

Exemplar Answers for Postassessment for the Change Concept

Note: Student answers may vary; these are simply to provide samples of quality postassessment answers to aid in scoring.

High Score

1. Give as many examples of things that change as you can (up to 10).
   Plants, People, Hair, Houses, Weather, Water, Soil, Animals, Paper, Crayons
2. Draw one example of something that changes, showing before and after.
   Before: Sunny weather; After: Rainy weather.
3. Identify five ways that a tree could change or be changed.
   Cut down, Poisoned, Leaves turn color, Leaves fall off, Rat
4. What are three things you can say about *all* change?
   Happens at different times. Has a meaning for happening. Is good or bad.

Medium Score

1. Give as many examples of things that change as you can (up to 10).
   Frogs, Children, Plants, People, Animals, Trees, Birds, Larva, Moth, Hair, Butterfly
2. Draw one example of something that changes, showing before and after.
   Before: Egg; After: Bird
3. Identify five ways that a tree could change or be changed.
   Colors of leaves
4. What are three things you can say about *all* change?
   Butterflies change from a caterpillar. Frogs change from a tadpole. Flowers are seeds first, then it is a flower.

Low Score

1. Give as many examples of things that change as you can (up to 10).
   Tree, wood
2. Draw one example of something that changes, showing before and after.
   Before: Tree; After: Paper
3. Identify five ways that a tree could change or be changed.
   Firewood, cut
4. What are three things you can say about *all* change?
   (Left blank)

Postassessment for Key Science Concepts

Directions to the Teacher: Read the following paragraph to students.

> Today I would like you to think about all of the things you know about soil. Think about the words you would use and the pictures you could draw to make a concept map. Think about the connections you can make. On your concept map paper, draw in pictures and words that you know about soil. You will be drawing a concept map similar to those you have done previously. The subject of your concept map is: "Tell me everything you know about soil."

Name:____________________ Date: ____________

Handout 17B
Concept Map: Soil

Exemplar Concept Maps of Soil for Postassessment for Key Science Concepts

High Score

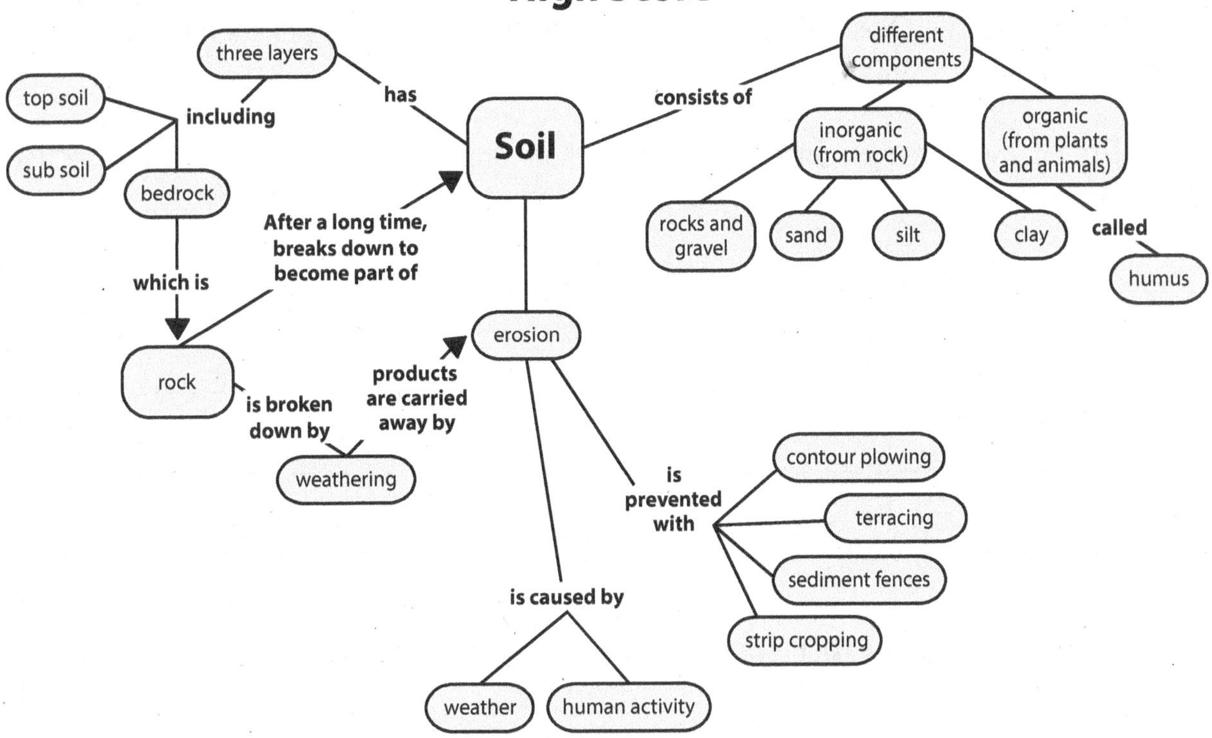

Medium Score

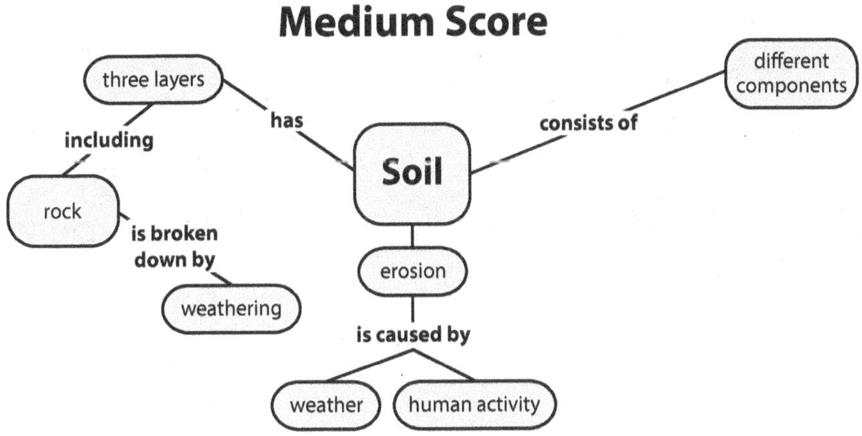

Low Score

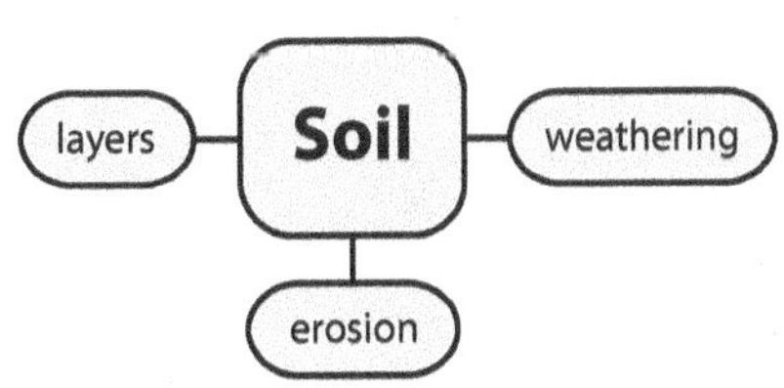

Name:____ Date: __________________

Handout 17C
Postassessment for Scientific Process

Directions: How would you study the question: How much water do plants need? Describe an experiment to test this question that includes the following:

1. Prediction regarding the question (How much water do plants need?):

   I predict that ____

   ____

   ____

   ____

2. What materials will be needed to conduct the experiment?

   ________________________ ________________________

   ________________________ ________________________

   ________________________ ________________________

3. What steps must be taken to conduct the experiment and in what order?

   a. ____

   b. ____

   c. ____

   d. ____

   e. ____

4. What data do you want to collect and how should they be recorded?

What will I collect?	How will I record the data?

5. How do the data help me decide if my prediction is correct? Explain.

____

____

____

____

Exemplar Answers for Postassessment for the Scientific Process

Note: Student answers may vary; these are simply to provide samples of quality postassessment answers to aid in scoring.

High Score

1. Prediction regarding the question (How much water do plants need?):
   I predict that you should give them about 2 cups every week.
2. What materials will be needed to conduct the experiment?
   Plant, sunlight, soil, fresh air, water, measuring cup
3. What steps must be taken to conduct the experiment and *in what order*?
   (a) Put a plant in soil. (b) Water it. (c) Put it in the sun. (d) Let it be in fresh air. (e) Water it every week.
4. What data do you want to collect and how should they be recorded?
   What will I collect? If I was right, I need more or less water in a certain amount of time. *How will I record the data?* In a log.
5. How do the data help me decide if my prediction is correct? Explain.
   If the plant is still alive.

Medium Score

1. Prediction regarding the question (How much water do plants need?):
   I predict that about 2 cups a day.
2. What materials will be needed to conduct the experiment?
   Soil, water, charts, magnifying glass
3. What steps must be taken to conduct the experiment and *in what order*?
   (a) Get the soil. (b) Get the water. (c) Collect the data. (d) Write it down. (e) Share your data.
4. What data do you want to collect and how should they be recorded?
   What will I collect? How much water will be needed? What kind of soil? *How will I record the data?* Notebook.
5. How do the data help me decide if my prediction is correct? Explain.
   Research on the computer, science books.

Low Score

1. Prediction regarding the question (How much water do plants need?):
   I predict that not that much of a whole lot of water.
2. What materials will be needed to conduct the experiment?
   Water, sunlight, topsoil, seeds, garden, nurturer
3. What steps must be taken to conduct the experiment and *in what order*?
   (a) First seeds to plant. (b) Then soil to help the plant. (c) Then sunlight. (d) Water. (e) Then cure.
4. What data do you want to collect and how should they be recorded?
   What will I collect? How much water plants need. *How will I record the data?* Science board.
5. How do the data help me decide if my prediction is correct? Explain.
   Give water. Water by day.

Part Three: Appendices

Appendix A
Concept Paper on Change

By Beverly T. Sher, Ph.D.

This paper was adapted from: Sher, B. T. (2004). Change. In J. L. VanTassel-Baska (Ed.), *Science key concepts* (pp. 31–35). Williamsburg, VA: Center for Gifted Education, The College of William and Mary.

We live in a changing world. Change and the absence of change are important features of both scientific and nonscientific processes. Change can occur in simple, predictable ways: Winter gradually gives way to spring, water evaporates from puddles after the rain ends, the sun rises and sets, we (well, most of us, anyway) change from a state of sleep at night to being awake in the daytime. It also can occur in more complicated and unpredictable ways: Hemlines rise and fall apparently randomly, the stock market gyrates, mutations resulting in changed organisms occur, the weather changes. It can also fail to occur: A bottle of root beer in the pantry, when opened, contains the same amount of liquid that it had months earlier at the bottling plant; healthy people maintain roughly the same body temperature at all times (with small, cyclic, daily variations); a rock formation photographed a year ago has the same contours now as it did then. In this concept paper, we will explore the concept of change and the related concept of equilibrium.

There are four general patterns of change. They include:

1. Steady changes: changes that occur at a characteristic rate.
2. Cyclic changes: changes that repeat in cycles.
3. Random changes: changes that occur irregularly, unpredictably, and in a way that is mathematically random.
4. Chaotic changes: changes that appear random and irregular on the surface, but are in fact predictable (in principle).

The first type of change is steady change. Change of this sort occurs at a predictable rate. For example, radioactive decay follows a predictable exponential curve. The number of undecayed atoms remaining after a given time in a radioactive sample can be simply calculated if one knows the half-life of the element involved. For example, half of the atoms in any sample will decay in 14.3 days. Similarly, the distance traveled by a car traveling at 55 miles an hour can be simply calculated for any time after the car leaves (assuming it hasn't run out of gas). Another familiar nonscientific example of steady change would be the steady growth of the balance in an untouched savings account: The rules of compound interest acting on the original balance produce a predictable growth in the daily balance of the account.

The second type of change, cyclic change, frequently is found in nature. A partial list of scientifically interesting cycles would include the phases of the moon, the sunspot cycle, the tides, daily cyclic changes in the levels of hormones in the human body, the sleep-wake cycle in animals, and so on. Some of these examples are familiar to nonscientists as well: We all expect the sun to rise in the east and set in the west once a day, and monthly variations in hormone levels have manifestations that are familiar to almost every female human being over the age of about 13. Other familiar cycles include the credit card billing cycle and the annual recurrence of events such as Christmas, Easter, and fund drives on public television.

The third type of change, random change, also is common in nature. Scientific examples would include the occurrence of spontaneous mutations in genes and the radioactive decay of individual atoms. Nobody can predict when a particular gene in a particular organism will undergo mutation, and nobody can tell by looking at a radioactive atom when it will decay. Interestingly enough, though, these processes that are random at the level of the individual gene or atom have definable rates when one looks at all of the genes in a population of animals (the mutation rate) or all of the radioactive atoms in a sample (the half-life). A similar, nonscientific, example would be winning the lottery. Winning the lottery is a random event. Beforehand, nobody can predict who will win; yet the odds of winning are predictable. Again, this is a process that is unpredictable at the individual level but totally predictable at the level of a population of individuals.

One of the most exciting developments in science in the 1980s was the understanding of chaotic change. Chaos occurs when a system obeys completely predictable behavior (i.e., given the exact state of a system at one time, one can determine its exact state at a future time), but our intrinsic lack of knowledge of its initial state causes its future behavior to appear random. Consider the motion of an asteroid, for example. If you knew the exact position and velocity of an asteroid, you could determine its exact position and velocity at any time in the future. However, a small uncertainty (such as a one millimeter uncertainty in its position) will eventually lead to a huge uncertainty in the future. The position of the asteroid in the future will not be determinable, that is, it will appear random. Similarly, if the location of all of the atoms of our atmosphere were perfectly known at one particular time, the weather could be predicted far into the future. The fact that we don't know those locations exactly (e.g., a butterfly flapping its wings in China will disturb some of the atoms) will lead to huge uncertainties in weather prediction; thus, we will likely never be able to predict the weather very far in advance. It might seem that it is difficult to differentiate between random change and chaotic change, but there are very precise mathematical relations followed by chaotic systems. One of the main realizations of the 1980s was that many systems previously thought to be random, such as water turbulence, weather phenomena, and even cardiac ventricular fibrillation, are in fact chaotic. A good nonscientific example of a chaotic process is the stock market's behavior.

Some systems are characterized not by change but by lack of change. These systems are said to be in equilibrium. The unopened bottle of soda on the shelf in the pantry illustrates this concept in several ways. First, it is static, at rest. All of the outside forces acting on it are balanced: Gravity pulling downward on it is balanced by the force that the shelf exerts to hold it up. Second, the amount of water in it is the same as the amount of water placed in it at the bottling plant. The water in the root beer is not static, however, but is in a state of dynamic equilibrium between two phases: water vapor in the little air space in the neck of the bottle and liquid water in the soda below. The important thing that allows this system to remain in equilibrium is that the bottle is closed. When it is closed, the average number of water molecules that evaporate and leave the liquid phase is exactly balanced by the average number of water molecules condensing from the vapor phase into the liquid phase. Once the bottle is opened, this equilibrium vanishes: Water molecules in the vapor phase can and do escape out the neck of the bottle and the water in the bottle will eventually evaporate. In dynamic equilibrium, therefore, a seeming lack of change reflects balanced processes of change occurring within a system.

The state of dynamic equilibrium that exists in a closed root beer bottle does not depend on any outside forces for its maintenance. Other examples of lack of change, though, represent the interposition of regulatory forces on the system. A simple example of such a system is the thermostat-house system. When the temperature in the house drops below a predetermined level, the sensor in the thermostat notices this and causes the furnace to heat the house. Once the house is warm again, the sensor in the thermostat causes the furnace to shut off. The maintenance of a constant temperature in the house is thus dependent on the regulatory behavior of the sensor. Feedback from the sensor keeps the system stable.

Another, more complicated example of regulated constancy is homeostasis: the maintenance of physical stability within an organism. In humans, for example, everything from our body temperature to the concentrations of different ions in our bloodstream remains fairly constant. This reflects tight control exerted by the cells of our body over these systems: regulation that requires constant sensing of the current state of affairs and compensation for changes that occur as we move, eat, sleep, and do all of the other things that humans do. One example of the mechanisms involved in homeostasis is the action of insulin and its function in regulating blood sugar levels. As a carbohydrate-rich meal begins to be absorbed by the body, the amount of glucose in the bloodstream begins to rise. In response to this, insulin is secreted by the pancreas into the bloodstream. Insulin stimulates the liver to take up extra sugar and store it in the form of glycogen (a starch-like substance); it increases the uptake of sugar by muscle cells and its conversion into glycogen; it inhibits the liver from producing glucose from its glycogen stores; and it stimulates muscle and liver cells to "burn" glucose for energy at a more rapid rate. These activities reduce the amount of glucose in the bloodstream, insulin secretion by the pancreas drops, and things are back to normal. The control of blood sugar levels by the body is complicated and requires a great deal of coordination among the different cells of the body.

Rationale for Teaching the Concept

Change is an inescapable feature of both scientific and nonscientific systems; indeed, it is often the most interesting feature of either kind of system. In science, for example, the study of developmental biology is concerned entirely with the mechanisms behind the amazing changes that occur as an organism develops from seed or fertilized egg into its mature form; meteorology concerns itself with atmospheric changes; and much of geology involves the study of the changes that have occurred since the Earth was formed. Outside of science, the daily changes in the stock market are important to millions of investors; changes in the weather matter to essentially everyone; and the changes that occur as a baby grows into an adult fascinate parents, grandparents, and teachers alike. An understanding of the basic types of change, as well as of the concept of equilibrium, is useful for anyone.

Suggested Applications

Many areas of science involve change. Below is a very partial list of suggestions for areas that could be used in illustrating change, equilibrium, and regulation.

Steady Change

Simple physical changes:

- Temperature change in water as it is heated (and what do you see at the freezing and boiling points?)
- Titration of an acid with a base; watch the pH change
- Rates of random change (mutation formation, radioactive decay)

Cyclic Change

- Astronomical phenomena (phases of the moon, seasons, changes in day length over the course of the year, behavior of the tides)
- Biological cycles (life cycles, sleep-wake cycle, opening and closing of flowers in plants over the course of the day, the turning of sunflowers to follow the sun, the menstrual cycle)

Random Change

- Radioactive decay
- Spontaneous mutation formation in microbes and man
- Study of probability and statistics

Chaotic Change

As discussed above, chaotic change is change that could in principle be predicted but in fact is unpredictable because of the large numbers of variables involved and uncertainty in measuring starting conditions. Younger children probably have enough difficulty learning that change can be predicted (steady change, cyclic change, rates of random change); introducing chaos at the same time might be confusing. For older children (grades 6–8 or so), the best introduction to chaos would probably be to play with a calculator or computer: Once they have seen the concept in this abstract way, they'll be able to see it in more concrete ways (one of the few cases where hands-on experimentation may *not* be the best way to introduce a new concept!).

Feedback, Control, and Regulation

- Electronics: study systems like thermostats
- Physiology (human and animal)

Appendix B
Teaching Models

Introduction to the Teaching Models

Several teaching models are incorporated into the Project Clarion units. These models ensure emphasis on unit outcomes and support student understanding of the concepts and processes that are the focus of each unit. Teachers should become familiar with these models and how to use them before teaching the unit. The models are listed below and outlined in the pages that follow.

1. Frayer Model of Vocabulary Development
2. Taba Model of Concept Development
3. Concept Mapping
4. Wheel of Scientific Investigation and Reasoning

Frayer Model of Vocabulary Development

The Frayer Model (Frayer, Frederick, & Klausmeier, 1969) provides students with a graphic organizer that asks them to think about and describe the meaning of a word or concept. This process enables them to strengthen their understanding of vocabulary words. Through the model, students are required to consider the important characteristics of the word and to provide examples and nonexamples of the concept. This model has similarities to the Taba Model of Concept Development (1962).

In introducing the Frayer Model to your students, demonstrate its use on large chart paper. Begin with a word all students know, such as rock, umbrella, or shoe, placing it on the graphic model. First, ask the students to define the word in their own words. Record a definition that represents their common knowledge. Next, ask students to give specific characteristics of the word/concept or facts they know about it. Record these ideas. Then ask students to offer examples of the idea and then nonexamples to finish the graphic (see Figure B1).

Another way to use the Frayer Model is to provide students with examples and nonexamples and ask them to consider what word or concept is being analyzed. You can provide similar exercises by filling in some portions of the graphic and asking students to complete the remaining sections.

As students share ideas, note the level of understanding of the group and of individual students. As the unit is taught, certain vocabulary words may need this type of expanded thinking to support student readiness for using the vocabulary in the science activities. You may want students to maintain individual notebooks of words so that they can refer back to them in their work.

Taba Model of Concept Development

Each Project Clarion unit supports the development of a specific macroconcept (change or systems). The concept development model, based upon the work of Hilda Taba (1962), supports student learning of the macroconcept. The model involves both inductive and deductive reasoning processes. Used as an early lesson in the unit, the model focuses on the creation of generalizations about the macroconcept from a

Definition	Characteristics (What a Scientist Does . . .)
"a person who studies nature and the physical world by testing, experimenting, and measuring"	• Ask questions. • Make observations. • Make predictions and/or hypotheses. • Collect, classify, and analyze data. • Design experiments. • Draw inferences. • Communicate findings.
Scientists	
Examples	**Nonexamples**
• Astronomers—study the universe (planets, stars, etc.) • Biologists—study life (plants and animals) • Geologists—study the Earth's layers of soil and rocks • Physicists—study matter and energy	• An entertainer • A poet • A banker

Figure B1. Completed graphic organizer for Frayer Model.

student-derived list of created concept examples. The model includes a series of steps, in which each step involves student participation. Students begin with a broad concept, determine specific examples of the broad concept, create appropriate categorization systems, cite nonexamples of the concept, establish generalizations based on their understanding, and then apply the generalizations to their readings and other situations.

The model generally is most effective when small groups of students work through each step, with whole-class debriefing following each stage of the process. However, with primary-age students, additional teacher guidance may be necessary, especially for the later stages of the model. The steps of the model are outlined below, using the unit concept of change.

1. Students generate examples of the concept of change, derived from their own understanding and experiences with change in the world. Teachers should encourage students to provide at least 15–20 examples; a class list may be created out of the small-group lists to lengthen the set of changes students have to work with.
2. Students then group their changes into categories. This process allows students to search for interrelatedness and to organize their thinking. It often is helpful to have individual examples written on cards so that the categorization may occur physically as well as mentally or in writing. Students should then explain their reasoning for their categorization system and seek clarification from each other as a whole group. Teachers should ensure that all examples have been accounted for in the categorization system established.
3. Students then generate a list of nonexamples of the concept of change. Teachers may begin this step with the direction, "Now list examples of things that *do not change.*" Encourage students to think carefully about their nonexamples and discuss ideas within their groups. Each group should list five to six nonexamples.

4. The students next determine generalizations about the concept of change, using their lists of examples, categories, and nonexamples. Teachers should then share the unit generalizations and relate valid student generalizations to the unit list. Both lists should be posted in the room throughout the course of the unit.
5. During the unit, students are asked to identify specific examples of the generalizations from their own readings, or to describe how the concept applies to a given situation about which they have read. Students also are asked to apply the generalizations to their own writings and their own lives. Several lessons employ a chart that lists several of the generalizations and asks students to supply examples specifically related to the reading or activity of that lesson.

Concept Mapping

A concept map is a graphic representation of one's knowledge on a particular topic. Concept maps support learning, teaching, and evaluation (Novak & Gowin, 1984). Students clarify and extend their own thinking about a topic. Teachers find concept mapping useful for envisioning the scope of a lesson or unit. They also use student-developed concept maps as a way of measuring their progress. Meaningful concept maps often begin with a particular question (focus question) about a topic, event, or object.

Concept maps were developed in 1972 by Dr. Joseph Novak at Cornell University as part of his research about young children's understanding of science concepts. Students were interviewed by researchers who recorded their responses. The researchers sought an effective way to identify changes in students' understanding over time. Novak and his research colleagues began to represent the students' conceptual understanding in concept maps because learning takes place through the assimilation of new concepts and propositions into existing conceptual and propositional frameworks.

Concept maps show concepts and relationships between them. (See the sample concept map in Figure B2.) The concepts are contained within boxes or oval shapes and the connections between concepts are represented by lines with linking words.

Concepts are the students' perceived ideas generalized from particular experiences. Sometimes the concepts placed on the map may contain more than one word. Words placed on the line link words or phrases. The propositions contain two or more concepts connected by linking words or phrases to form a meaningful statement.

The youngest students may view and develop concept maps making basic connections. They may begin with two concepts joined by a linking word. These "sentences" (propositions) become the building blocks for concept maps. Older students may begin to make multiple connections immediately as they develop their maps.

As students map their knowledge base, they begin to represent their conceptual understanding in a hierarchical manner. The broadest, most inclusive concepts often are found at the top of a concept map. More specific concepts and examples then follow.

Each Project Clarion unit contains an overview concept map, showing the essential knowledge included in the lessons and the connections students should be able to make as a result of their experiences within the unit. This overview may be useful as a classroom poster that the teacher and students may refer to throughout the unit.

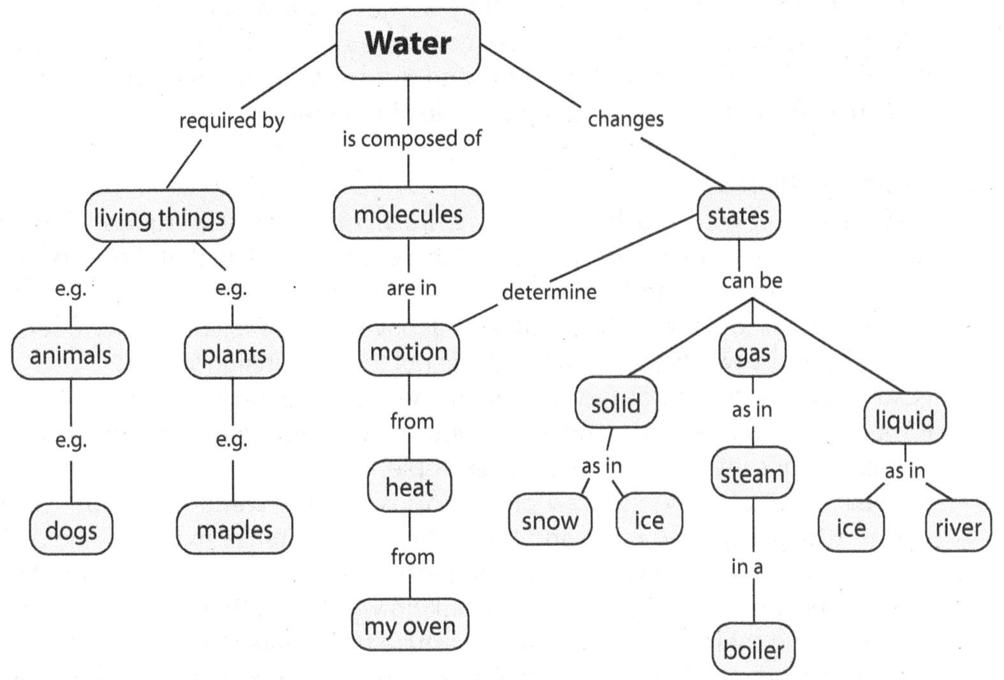

Figure B2. A concept map showing a student's understanding of water.
Note. Adapted from Novak and Gowin (1984).

Strategies to Prepare Students for Concept Mapping

The following strategies can be incorporated to help prepare your students for concept mapping activities (Novak & Gowin, 1984).

What Do Words Mean?

1. Ask students to picture in their minds some common words (e.g., water, tree, door, box, pencil, dog). Start with "object" words, saying them one at a time, allowing time for students to picture each of them.
2. Create a class list of object words, asking students to name other objects they can picture in their minds to add to the list.
3. Next, create a list of event words (e.g., jumping, running, eating). Ask students to envision each of these in their minds and encourage them to contribute to the class list of event words.
4. Give students a few words that are likely to be unfamiliar to most of them, asking if they can see a picture in their mind. These words should be short (e.g., data, cell, prey, inertia). You might include a few simple words in another language. Ask students if they have any mind pictures.
5. Discuss the fact that words are useful to us because they convey meaning. This only happens when people can form a picture in their mind that represents the meaning they connect with the word.

What Is a Concept?

1. Introduce the word *concept* and explain that concept is the word we use to mean some kind of object or event we can picture in our mind. Refer back to the word lists previously developed as you discuss the word and ask if these are concepts. Can students see a picture in their mind for each of them? Let students know

that when they come upon a word they do not know well enough to form a picture, they will just need to learn the concept associated with that new word.

2. Provide each table with picture cards and ask students to take turns at their table naming some of the concepts included in the card.

What Are Linking Words?

1. Prepare a list of words such as *the, is, are, when, that, then*. Ask students if they can see a picture in their mind for each of these words. Explain that these are not concept words. These are linking words we use when we speak or write to link concept words together into sentences that have special meaning. Ask students if they have any words to add to the list. Label the list "Linking Words."
2. Hold up two picture cards (sky and blue) and give students a sample sentence ("The sky is blue.") Ask students to tell you the concept words and the linking words in your sentence. Give another example.
3. Give each pair of students a few picture cards. Ask the students to work with partners to pick up two cards and then develop a sentence that links the two cards. They should take turns, with one partner making the sentence and the other identifying the concepts and the linking words. Ask them to repeat this a few times and then have several partners share their sentences.
4. Explain to students that it is easy to make up sentences and to read sentences where the printed labels (words) are familiar to them. Explain that reading and writing sentences is like making a link between two things (concepts) they already know. Practice this idea during reading time, asking students to find a sentence and analyze it for concepts and linking words.

Wheel of Scientific Investigation and Reasoning

All scientists work to improve our knowledge and understanding of the world. In the process of scientific inquiry, scientists connect evidence with logical reasoning. Scientists also apply their imaginations as they devise hypotheses and explanations that make sense of the evidence. Students can strengthen their understanding of particular science topics through investigations that cause them to employ evidence gathering, logical reasoning, and creativity. The Wheel of Scientific Investigation and Reasoning contains the specific processes involved in scientific inquiry to guide students' thinking and actions.

Make Observations

Scientists make careful observations and try things out. They must describe things as accurately as possible so that they can compare their observations from one time to another and so that they can compare their observations with those of other scientists. Scientists use their observations to form questions for investigation.

Ask Questions

Scientific investigations usually are initiated through a problem to be solved or a question asked. Selecting just the right question or clearly defining the problem to be addressed is critical to the investigation process.

Learn More

To clarify their questions, scientists learn more by reviewing bodies of scientific knowledge documented in text and previously conducted investigations. Also, when scientists get conflicting information they make fresh observations and insights that may result in revision of the previously formed question. By learning more, scientists can design and conduct more effective experiments or build upon previously conducted experiments.

Design and Conduct the Experiment

Scientists use their collection of relevant evidence, their reasoning, and their imagination to develop a hypothesis. Sometimes scientists have more than one possible explanation for the same set of observations and evidence. Often when additional observations and testing are completed, scientists modify current scientific knowledge.

To test out hypotheses, scientists design experiments that will enable them to control conditions so that their results will be reliable. Scientists repeat their experiments, doing it the same way it was done before and expecting to get very similar, although not exact, results. It is important to control conditions in order to make comparisons. Scientists sometimes are not sure what will happen because they don't know everything that might be having an effect on the experiment's outcome.

Create Meaning

Scientists analyze the data that are collected from the experiment to add to the existing body of scientific knowledge. They organize their data using data tables and graphs and then make inferences from the data to draw conclusions about whether their question was answered and the effectiveness of their experiments. Scientists also create meaning by comparing what they found to existing knowledge. The analysis of data often leads to identification of related questions and future experiments.

Tell Others What Was Found

In the investigation process, scientists often work as a team, sharing findings with each other so that they may benefit from the results. Initially, individual team members complete their own work and draw their own conclusions.

One way to introduce the wheel to students is to provide them with the graphic model (see Figure B3) and ask them to tell one reason why each section of the wheel is important to scientific investigation.

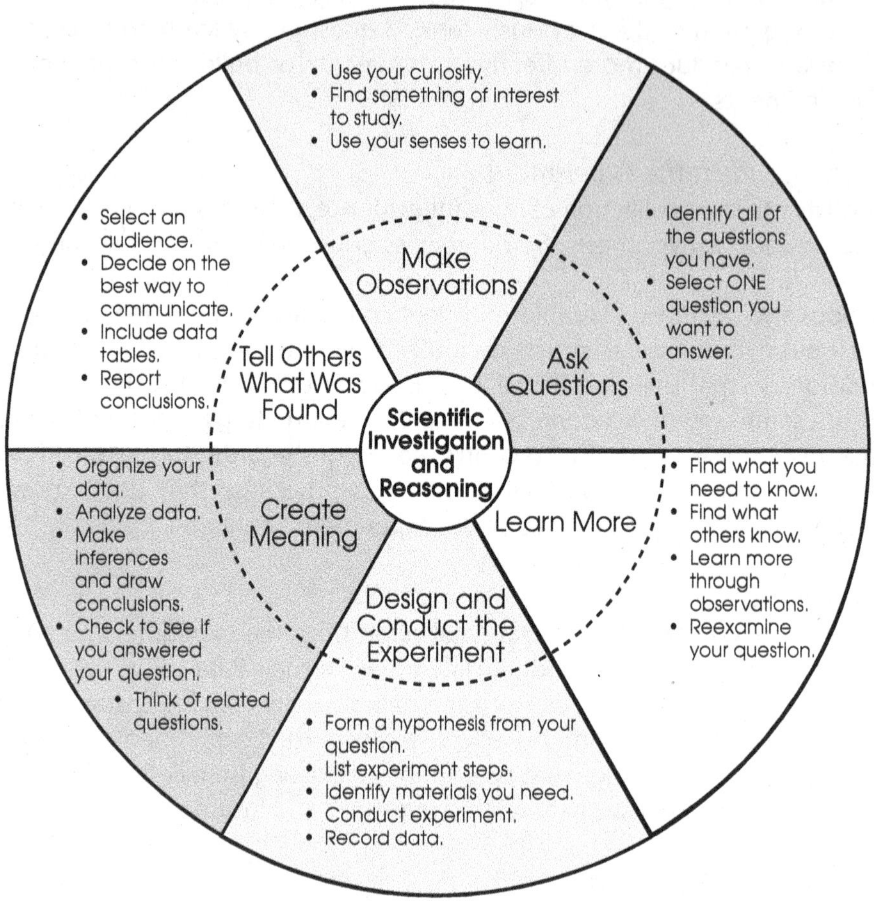

Figure B3. Wheel of Scientific Investigation and Reasoning model.
Note. Adapted from Kramer (1987).

Appendix C
Materials List

Lesson	Materials
Lesson 1: Preassessment	Copies of preassessments for unit concept, process, and content Pencils Student Logs – spiral or composition notebooks Rubric/scoring guide for preassessments (Teacher Resource) Preteaching for Key Science Concepts Preassessment Instructions (Teacher Resource) Copy of Sample Concept Map (Teacher Resource) Large chart paper Drawing paper for each student
Lesson 2: What Is a Scientist?	Lab coat for teacher One lab coat (white adult T-shirt or dress shirt) for each student Beaker Microscope Prepared slides or transparencies of Handouts 2A and 2B One copy of Handout 2A for each group of three or four students Markers or pens One piece of chart paper Student logs Blank nametags
Lesson 3: The Concept of Change	Chart paper for each group of 4 students with Taba Concept Model Chart for students to complete One pack of sticky notes per group of three to four students Markers Four sentence strips with a different change generalization written on each strip Student logs Large Taba Concept Model Chart for the class Examples of erosion and weathering, either physical objects or photographs. Images should include examples students will be familiar with, such as from the local area, and other images. Examples can be found at: http://science.nationalgeographic.com/science/photos/weathering-erosion-gallery/#, http://www.teachersdomain.org/asset/ess05_img_erosion/, or http://geology.about.com/od/geoprocesses/ig/mechweathering/. Story about the collapse of Utah's "Wall Arch" at Arches National Park with before and after pictures: http://www.nps.gov/arch/parknews/news080808.htm.

Lesson	Materials
Lesson 4: Becoming a Geologist	Projector and screen Online access to http://kids.earth.nasa.gov/archive/career/geologist.html, http://www.agiweb.org/workforce/brochure.html (Optional) "So you want to be a Geologist" (http://youtu.be/XVfkP0kuyog): a 2-minute video from http://www.aie.org that explains what geologists do. (Optional) "Careers in Geology" (http://youtu.be/UZR8MiTJDA0): an episode of the television program *On The Job* that highlights careers in geology that is made available by the University of Alabama. (Optional) "Why I Became a Geologist" (http://youtu.be/Feq5pwH2TFw): a one-minute video from the Environmental Science Institute in which Dr. Randy Marrett explains why he became a geologist. Markers or pens Student logs Handout 4A Copy of Handout 4B to project onscreen
Lesson 5: Rock Detectives	Computer with access to Internet Projector and screen Markers or pens for students Student logs Samples of rocks (one type per group) Set A: obsidian, basalt, and granite (igneous), Set B: limestone, shale, coal, and sandstone (sedimentary), Set C: quartzite, slate, marble, and gneiss (metamorphic) Magnifying glasses (one per student) Crayons and colored pencils Handouts 5A–5D
Lesson 6: Changing Rocks	Collection of rocks Sugar cubes Books about rocks and minerals (see Student Resources on p. 11 for suggestions) Plastic fillable eggs Pieces of chalk Vinegar Small plastic bottle with cap Rocks Water Wood Freezer Handouts 6A–6E

Lesson	Materials
Lesson 6: Changing Rocks, *continued*	Safety goggles (for Station 5) Jars labeled A and B Steel file Pieces of limestone or hard candies Sandpaper (fine, medium, rough) Newspaper or disposable table cloth Sponge Student logs
Lesson 7: Soil Formation	Access to the Internet Computer with projector and speakers Handout of soil formation information (four copies separated by group) Handout 7A and 7B Plastic bags (two per student) Student logs
Lesson 8: Components of Soil	Students' soil samples Plastic plates (one per soil sample) Newspaper to cover the table One small bag, per group, of the following: Sand Clay (can use modeling clay if necessary) Silt (can use chalk dust as substitute if necessary) Rocks and gravel Humus (compost) Handout 8A Magnifying glasses (one for each group, if possible) Student logs
Lesson 9: Soil Horizons	Access to the Internet One small bag, per group, of the following: Sand Clay (can use modeling clay if necessary) Silt (can use chalk dust as substitute if necessary) Rocks and gravel Humus (compost) Mason jar (one per group) Magnifying glasses (one for each group, if possible) Shovel/spade (one per group) White paper (one piece for each group) Measuring tape (one per group)

Lesson	Materials
Lesson 9: Soil Horizons, *continued*	White glue (one bottle for each group) Handout 9A Student logs
Lesson 10: Plants and Soil	Access to the Internet Sample of gravel, clay, sand, silt, and humus per group Four wide mouth jars per group Filter paper Plastic pitcher of water (one per group) Graduated cylinder (one per group) 1/4 measuring cup (one per group) Potted plant in clear container (for demo) Large jar (for demo) Small spade Student logs
Lesson 11: Erosion	Old paint roller trays or 9"x13" baking sheets Soil Soil with grass growing in it Objects to use as barriers to erosion (e.g., compost, mulch, twigs, popsicle sticks, toothpicks) Hair dryer Water cans filled with water Water source Student logs
Lesson 12: Erosion as Change	Chart paper for each student Markers
Lesson 13: Erosion Prevention	Handouts 13A and 13B
Lesson 14: Contemporary Issue: Fracking	Video: "Fracking: Positive or Negative Impact?": http://www.pbs.org/newshour/spc/thenews/foreducators/story.php?id=19829&package_id=634 Internet and print resources about fracking
Lesson 15: Persuasive Writing	Handout 15A Paper and pencils Student logs
Lesson 16: Putting it All Together	Chart paper Markers
Lesson 17: Postassessment	Exemplar answers (Teacher Resource) Copies of postassessments Pencils

References

Frayer, D. A., Frederick, W. C., & Kausmeier, H. J. (1969). *A schema for testing the level of concept mastery*. Working paper from the Wisconsin Research and Development Center for Cognitive Learning, The University of Wisconsin.

Kramer, S. P. (1987). *How to think like a scientist: Answering questions by the scientific method*. New York, NY: T. Y. Crowell.

Novak, J., & Gowin, B. D. (1984). *Learning how to learn*. New York, NY: Cambridge University Press.

Scholastic. (1996). *Scholastic children's dictionary* (Rev. ed.). New York, NY: Author.

Sher, B. T. (2004). Change. In J. L. VanTassel-Baska (Ed.), *Science key concepts* (pp. 31–35). Williamsburg, VA: Center for Gifted Education, College of William and Mary.

Taba, H. (1962). *Curriculum: Theory and practice*. New York, NY: Harcourt Brace.

United States Environmental Protection Agency. (2013). *The process of hydraulic fracturing*. Retrieved from http://www2.epa.gov/hydraulicfracturing/process-hydraulic-fracturing

VanTassel-Baska, J. (1986). Effective curriculum and instructional models for talented students. *Gifted Child Quarterly, 30,* 164–169.

VanTassel-Baska, J., & Little, C. (Eds.). (2003). *Content-based curriculum for gifted learners*. Waco, TX: Prufrock Press.

References

Next Generation Science Standards Alignment

Lesson	Next Generation Science Standards
Preteaching Lesson–Lesson 4	N/A
Lesson 5	MS-ESS2-1: Develop a model to describe the cycling of Earth's materials and the flow of energy that drives this process.
Lesson 6	4-ESS2-1: Make observations and/or measurements to provide evidence of the effects of weathering or the rate of erosion by water, ice, wind, or vegetation.
Lesson 7	4-ESS2-1: Make observations and/or measurements to provide evidence of the effects of weathering or the rate of erosion by water, ice, wind, or vegetation.
Lesson 8	4-ESS2-1: Make observations and/or measurements to provide evidence of the effects of weathering or the rate of erosion by water, ice, wind, or vegetation.
Lesson 9	4-ESS2-1: Make observations and/or measurements to provide evidence of the effects of weathering or the rate of erosion by water, ice, wind, or vegetation.
Lesson 10	5-LS2-1: Develop a model to describe the movement of matter among plants, animals, decomposers, and the environment.
Lesson 11	4-ESS2-1: Make observations and/or measurements to provide evidence of the effects of weathering or the rate of erosion by water, ice, wind, or vegetation.
Lesson 12	4-ESS2-1: Make observations and/or measurements to provide evidence of the effects of weathering or the rate of erosion by water, ice, wind, or vegetation.
Lesson 13	5-ESS3-1: Obtain and combine information about ways individual communities use science ideas to protect the Earth's resources and environment.
Lesson 14	5-ESS3-1: Obtain and combine information about ways individual communities use science ideas to protect the Earth's resources and environment.
Lesson 15	5-ESS3-1: Obtain and combine information about ways individual communities use science ideas to protect the Earth's resources and environment.
Lessons 16–17	N/A